Dean Ann E. P. Mc Elliott *

D0194176

Sheer Christianity

January
2005

Sheer Christianity

Conjectures on a Catechism

Sam Portaro

COWLEY PUBLICATIONS
CAMBRIDGE, MASSACHUSETTS

Published in the United States of America by Cowley Publications, a
division of the Society of Saint John the Evangelist. No portion of this
book may be reproduced, stored in or introduced into a retrieval system,
or transmitted, in any form or by any means—including photocopying—
without the prior written permission of Cowley Publications, except in
the case of brief quotations embedded in critical articles and reviews.

Scripture quotations are taken from The New Revised Standard Version
of the Bible, © 1989, by the Division of Christian Education of the
National Council of the Churches of Christ in the United States of
America. Used by permission.

Library of Congress Cataloging-in-Publication Data
Portaro, Sam Anthony.
  Sheer Christianity : conjectures on a catechism / Sam Portaro.
     p. cm.
  Includes bibliographical references.
  ISBN 1-56101-268-8 (pbk. : alk. paper)
  1. Church of England–Catechisms. 2. Church of England–Doctrines.
I. Title.
  BX5139.P67 2004
  238'.3–dc22
                                                              2004018694

Cover design: Gary Ragaglia

This book was printed in Canada on acid-free paper.

Cowley Publications
4 Brattle Street
Cambridge, Massachusetts 02138
800-225-1534 • www.cowley.org

sheer *adjective* [from Middle English *schere* freed from guilt, probably alteration of *skere*, from Old Norse *skærr* pure; akin to Old English *scinan* to shine] **1:** *obsolete:* BRIGHT, SHINING **2:** of thin or transparent texture: DIAPHANOUS **3a:** UNQUALIFIED, UTTER (as in *sheer* folly) **b:** PURE, UNMIXED **c:** viewed or acting in dissociation from all else (won by *sheer* determination) **4:** PRECIPITOUS, PERPENDICULAR; **synonym:** STEEP *adverb* ALTOGETHER, COMPLETELY. *verb* (perhaps alteration of *shear*): to deviate from a course: SWERVE

Christianity *noun* **1:** the whole body of Christian believers **2:** the religion derived from Jesus Christ, based on the Bible as sacred scripture, and professed by Eastern, Roman Catholic, and Protestant bodies **3:** conformity to the Christian religion

conjecture *noun* [from Latin *conjectus*, literally, to throw together] SUPPOSITION; a conclusion derived by surmise or guesswork; implies basing an opinion or judgment upon evidence insufficient for definite knowledge; **synonym:** SURMISE implies even slighter evidence and suggests the influence of imagination or suspicion

catechism *noun* [from Greek *katechesis*, from *katechein* to teach] **1:** oral instruction **2:** a manual for catechizing: *specifically* a summary of religious doctrine, often in the form of questions and answers

—adapted from Merriam-Webster's Collegiate Dictionary, Tenth Edition

Contents

Note: All passages indicated in parentheses by *BCP* are taken from *The Book of Common Prayer*, 1979.

Introduction

SOME YEARS AGO I sat in a sunny room at Brent House with Joseph Kitagawa, then retired from his long tenure as professor and dean at the University of Chicago Divinity School. Enjoying the rare treat of conversation with this wise and fascinating priest and educator, I asked him what he thought the greatest challenge to Christians in our own day might be.

Christians, Joe replied, are quite skilled at telling their story to one another, but their language is the language of an insider culture. No one outside the culture understands what they're talking about. The greatest challenge for Christians will be translating their story into words those outside this closed society can understand.

That challenge is hardly unique to contemporary Christians. Telling our story in comprehensible language has been a constant task. Every generation struggles to convey to the next the stories that frame human experience, that give meaning to and make sense of our daily lives. Christians know this work by the name *evangelism*, the transmission of the good news—*evangelion* in Greek—to others.

I love stories and the words that make them. English was my undergraduate major. Of the classical languages of Christian biblical scholarship, Hebrew and Greek, I have only the most rudimentary knowledge. My own faith is deeply rooted in English texts, and I am deeply indebted to those gifted in "the interpretation of tongues" whose skill carefully and deliberately chose specific words to render ancient texts accessible in this language.

Throughout these pages that love will be apparent in my frequent use of the dictionary as a basic tool. Comprehending the riches of the biblical stories and making sense of my own experience demands a constant search for the riches buried in words. Every trip to the dictionary rewards me with new perspectives and an abiding appreciation for the elegance of language, the richest of all the earthen vessels we use to carry the treasure of God's truth through life and history.

In 1908, G. K. Chesterton published a slender volume somewhat immodestly entitled *Orthodoxy*. In the preface, he confessed that the work was autobiographical and "egotistical only in order to be sincere." A generation later, in 1952, C. S. Lewis gathered up three series of radio talks into the single volume *Mere Christianity*. Each of these works profoundly influenced me in my faith journey, and I am indebted both to their insights and their example, their example being at least one motivation for this offering.

As Christian believers Chesterton and Lewis understood their evangelical responsibility. Gifted writers, their calls and compulsions led them to the risky venture of putting their faith into words, and their words into print. Every spiritual journey is a personal quest. While the path may sometimes be shared with others, each must take his or her own steps.

The title of this book pays homage and risks comparison but, more important, is intentionally open to multiple meaning. The compelling beauty of the Christian faith is its transparency. Those who met Jesus in his own time, and those who encounter him yet today, profess to see ultimate truth. That this clarity is available to the simplest unschooled mind and the most complexly skeptical intellect, to the most eager spirit and the most hardened heart, only makes encounter with the Christ the more mysterious.

But every encounter with another compels response, for even to ignore or reject is a reply. When the one met is comprehended as the ultimate Other, as God, this responsibility may combine the exhilaration of steep ascent and precipitous danger. Hence, relationship with God—like any deep passion—is like the attraction of moth to flame. Drawn by the light and warmth, one is still aware of the threat of annihilation, of being totally consumed.

Yet we persist, drawn by the essence and dynamic of living relationship that is a not-knowing, the compulsion of curiosity that attends all mystery and sustains all relationship—religious, romantic, and real. Even when we think we know, we are never fully knowing—or known. Thus, all life is actually built upon faith—a constant and ongoing conjecture, a succession of tentative judgments made of partial knowledge, the only kind of knowledge humans are allowed. Aided by the divine gift of imagination and tempered by humble suspicion, we make our way in relationship from day to day in a process of continual learning.

I have sometimes suggested to friends, only partly in jest, that an apt epitaph for my gravestone would be "It was a valuable learning experience." Life is an unending search for meaning and, as my father has often said, the longer I live the more I discover how little I know. Yet, the way we "know" in relationship is quite different from the way we "know" the physical world around us. Our knowledge of the world is based on scientific method, on empirical experimentation and observation. Through tests, consistently repeated and measured, we can discern the elemental properties of much of the physical world. While our findings are always partial, temporary, and subject to alteration by future discoveries, we have obtained sufficient confidence in this knowledge to alter radically our stewardship of the earth and its resources. Knowledge of the essential properties of wood, metal, and stone has allowed us to shelter ourselves. Understanding the nature of fibers and the arts of fabrication has clothed us. Insights into propagation and agriculture now feed thousands off crops and acreage that once might only have sustained a hundred.

But to paraphrase the two fathers in *The Fantasticks*, when you plant a radish, a radish grows; but with children you don't know the result until long after the seed is sown. Human life and relationships are inconsistent, unpredictable. Nearly all that we know of one another, beyond our physical bodies, is intuitive and difficult, even impossible, to measure or quantify. We never truly "know" that we are loved, so much as we are encouraged to believe that we are loved, by another. The foundation of love in relationship is not affection, it is trust, faith.

So how does one teach faith? For that matter, how does one teach love, hope? If this trinity of cardinal theological virtues comprises the essence of Christian belief, then how does one teach Christianity? These are but a few of the questions that led our ancestors in faith and us, their inheritors, to devise catechisms.

Catechism is the Greek word for *teaching*. A catechism is *a* teaching, not necessarily *the* teaching, of a community of faith. The basis of every Christian catechism is questions. The questions chart relationship with God. Each question, like a locus on a map, may have multiple routes in and out, connecting each to God and often connecting one to another. Thus, just as it is nearly impossible for me to travel between home and office without crossing through certain communities or passing particular landmarks, it is nearly impossible to address any one question in a catechism without anticipating or participating in another.

For many years I have used the Catechism of the *Book of Common Prayer* as the outline for a conversational inquirers' class. As in any conversation, each section of the catechism and any question therein can lead to digression, launching interesting explorations down side roads whose routes pass through several sections of the larger outline. While we may not always reach a conclusive destination—an answer to a question upon which we can all agree—the journey itself is always worth the effort.

Because the route of my journey wound through the academic community, I have found "thesis" another helpful analogy to cate-chesis. A thesis begins with a hunch, a faith assertion. The work of the scholar is to examine that assertion thoroughly, challenging it, probing it in hope of affirming the assertion, disproving the proposition, or sometimes discovering another, more interesting—and possibly more valuable—insight. Both the catechetical and the scholarly journey require courage and faith, and whether searching for greater insight into an academic proposition, or seeking a deeper knowledge of and relationship with God, the desired outcome is truth.

The assertion that God is love, while certainly an encouragement, is not nearly so important in catechesis as the assertion that God is truth. If we believe God to be the source and end of all that is holy—the word *holy* itself being a synonym for *whole*—then God is ultimate truth. Truth is immutable. I do not make truth, I can only discover it. I cannot change truth, I can only stand in relation to it. Just as saying something is true doesn't make it so, conversely, to maintain that a truth is untrue does not make it so, either. Truth, then, is beyond my harm. It will withstand my questions, endure my assaults, and survive my denials. I am free to affirm or deny truth, but I cannot change or destroy it.

Furthermore, while the study of religion, of scripture and its languages, is an enhancement to the exploration of God's truth, access to God and God's truth is not denied those who approach with only native curiosity and everyday experience. Indeed, birth itself is our invitation to join the journey, and long before the tools of language, scholarly discourse, and academic research were discovered and developed, generations encountered and apprehended that truth of God, and God's truth.

Let me be clear at the outset that what I offer in the remaining pages is only one fleeting vantage on a continuing journey. All who undertake to explore and understand truth—who seek God—are constrained by experience and language. These are the limitations, and the gifts, of our finitude. These are the boundaries within which we operate. All explorations into truth are partial, limited, and temporary. No single experience shared by two people will be apprehended by each of them in exactly the same way. Two of us can stand before the same painting and see entirely different things. The painting is greater than what either of us sees, but it is also less—it is only pigment arranged on canvas until we meet it with our vision and experience and bring both to bear in our interpretation of what it means to us.

But no meaning I derive from the painting will alter the truth, the essential wholeness of its particular arrangement of pigment on canvas. That will remain the same for the artist and for each person who sees it. Analogy, metaphor, simile, and example are all necessary tools in catechesis.

If we agree at the outset that God is God, that God is who God is, and that whatever and whoever God is remain truth beyond our full comprehension, then we need all the help and hands we can muster, like the characters in the tale of the blind men and the elephant.

As the story goes, several blind men seek to describe an animal that happens to be an elephant. They surround the animal, and each one reaches out and touches it. After an interval, they begin to share. The one feeling the elephant's leg says, "The creature is like a tree, with a rough, solid trunk too large to reach all the way around." The one grasping the elephant's trunk says, "Ah, it is like a snake, long and sinuous." The one leaning forward with both hands flat against the elephant's side says, "It is like a vast wall, strong and immovable."

Each, of course, was correct, up to a point. Within the limits of each one's experience and evidence, the elephant was as described. But none of them knew the whole truth of the elephant. Yet, by adding their parts together, their partial experience and knowledge were enlarged and enriched. So it is with our catechetical journey, our lifelong process of relationship with God, our search for truth and meaning.

One thing more may be helpful to our exploration, and that is a word about the etiological nature of our search and learning. Etiology is the study of causes. My younger brother Dan was a dedicated etiologist. Give him a toy and he'd have it taken apart very quickly; he wanted to know what made it work.

Like Molière's *Bourgeois Gentilhomme*, who was delighted to discover that he spoke "prose" without knowing it, many of us practice etiology every day. A cook reasonably familiar with kitchen chemistry can recreate a recipe by working backwards. From a bite of rich, moist, dark chocolate cake, the cook knows that the cake probably has a large quantity of flour as a primary ingredient. The dark chocolate flavor suggests cocoa, and cocoa needs a pinch of salt to cut its bitterness, a bit of vanilla to enhance its depth. The sweetness indicates sugar, the moistness a quantity of oil, either vegetable or butter. Eggs provide a binder. With some experimentation, the cook will eventually discover the recipe, or even improve upon it. But the process is essentially the same, whether one is curious to know how a cake is made, or a universe.

Our ancestors in faith, seeking to know the causes of human life and experience, set down one of the earliest records of the search. What are we? How did we get here? Why are we here? From these questions they proceeded, and we persevere. Welcome to the journey.

1

Where to Begin

THE SEVENTEENTH-CENTURY British poet Alexander Pope advised, "Know then thyself, presume not God to scan, the proper study of mankind is Man." Thus the catechism of the *Book of Common Prayer* begins with what we know, which is ourselves. "What are we by nature?" it asks. How and why are we made?

The first explorations of a new infant seem to concentrate upon self-examination. Curious to explore its own body, a baby finds its mouth with tentative fingers, grabs toes and explores them. Not yet aware of what is happening in its body, yet ruled by its functions, a child seeks to know and must be taught what each pain or pleasure means. Why do I feel happy? Why do I feel sad or sick? What's happening to me, in me? Eventually comes the question, or some variation of it, "How was I made?"

The story of the world's creation, and Adam's, opens the biblical narrative. Yes, God is present, is even the principal character of the story. But there is no explanation of God. The focus is upon the world as we know it: Light and dark, time itself marked in day and night, earth, sky, and sea. The elemental forces of air, fire, water. Vegetation. Animals—aquatic, airborne, and amphibious. Creatures lithe and lumbering. But at the center of all, in the center of the garden, Adam. Then Eve.

Like the cook seeking to unravel the mystery of cake, the authors of Genesis begin with a literal slice of life, the world as they know it. They name our primal ancestor Adam, the Hebrew word for red clay, mud. Without any of the instruments of modern science, they discern that our physical bodies are intimately connected, even derived from, the elements of the earth itself. Perhaps because they know death, have watched bodies disintegrate in ash and earth, they deduce the connection. But for them it establishes a relationship and integrated wholeness with all the other elements of the created order. Subsequent science has not refuted their conjecture, but verifies it in the discovery that our bodies are largely water, the remaining ingredients all common to the ground beneath our feet or the seas that lap its shores.

Why are some humans made of one gender, others of another? Why male and female? Opinion was obviously divided. One author, grasping the leg of the animal, says the difference is necessary to reproduction. Another author, holding the trunk, declares that Eve was created as companion for Adam in order that he not be alone. Both are correct, but neither one nor the other, or even the combination of both perspectives, begins to approach the fullness of the mystery. As a beginning, however, the two perspectives and the inclusion of each in the narrative reflect both the progressive and the generous natures of our revelatory tradition.

What are we by nature? At base, we're a single species of differentiated but complementary gender capable of reproduction and fitted for social interdependence. That's a technical summary of the stories, but isn't the narrative more interesting, more creative? The story itself, then, is also part of the answer to the question "What are we by nature?" We are, by nature, imaginative storymakers, creative storytellers. We are capable of relating our lives and experiences to the world of which we're a part, and we can relate those stories to one another. Life doesn't merely happen to us. We are reflexive, reflective creatures. We can imagine, and we do.

Mark Twain once quipped that "God created man in his own image and man, being a gentleman, returned the compliment." It was not courtesy so much as necessity that moved our ancestors, and encourages us, to imagine God as being like us, and we like God. It's not arrogance, but poverty, that makes this act of imagination necessary. The limitations of our finitude and our language make imagination the only vehicle for our exploration. Like the blind characters of the elephant story, we have limited vision; the apostle Paul said as much in his first letter to the church in Corinth: "Now we see in a mirror dimly, but then we will see face to face. Now I know only in part, then I will know fully, even as I have been fully known" (13:12).

Now I have hold of only part of the elephant and can perceive it only by touch, see it only in my mind's eye. Now I have only that portion of God limited to my own particular experience, my own imagination, but my imagination is limited to my experience of this finite world. While I anticipate one day standing in God's presence, with eternity's depth and breadth available to sustain a more intimate and profound experience and knowledge of God, for now I have only analogy, metaphor, and simile to encompass and give expression to what I perceive of God in and through this world.

Still, I do have imagination. Though I do not know if other creatures possess this gift, it is mine. Experience thus far suggests that this gift of imagination is a particular trait of humans, and an essential characteristic of creativity. The Genesis story deduces that we humans are made to be companions and co-creators with God. Life doesn't just happen to us; we assist God in the making of life. In this way, it would seem, we are like God.

While I was privileged to grow up with full knowledge (or to whatever extent we can ever account knowledge as "full") of both my parents, when we set out to know God, we begin as metaphorical orphans. In the baptismal liturgy we affirm that we are a product of creation—a creature—a child of God. This principle is a fundament of Christian faith, a basic assumption upon which we rest our faith and against which we measure our experience. At the baptismal font, biological parents stand much as they did on their wedding day, but with a new life, a child, between them. Whatever else we understand to happen in that liturgy, this rite serves to remind both the mother and father, and we who form the extended family of community, that this child is more than the organic confluence of sperm, egg, and the favorable outcome of nine months' gestation. Biological mother and father humbly acknowledge that they, of their own accord, could not—did not—achieve this considerable miracle. They affirm that God cooperated in this creative act, that God is as much parent of this child as they are. This child, they vow, will be reared in the love and knowledge of this creative trinity.

The child's knowledge of God, however, is mediated in and through the finite, physical realm of human parents, of community, culture, and nature. We children of God are all, to some extent, like adoptees in search of our birth parent. We may know and love, respect and cherish the mother and father who surround us with love, who provide for our needs. But we live always with a hunger to know more deeply and profoundly that spiritual parent.

What does it mean to be created in the image of God? If we really are created by God, how can we and everything else in creation escape traces of the Creator? It is a consequence of creation that creators leave impressions. Jesus used this fundamental understanding of our creation in that clever and quick-witted response to the wag who goaded him with a dangerous question about taxes, authority, and loyalty.

> "Is it lawful for us to pay taxes to the emperor, or not?" But he perceived their craftiness and said to them, "Show me a denarius. Whose head and whose title does it bear?" They said, "The emperor's." He said to them, "Then give to the emperor the things that are the emperor's, and to God the things that are God's." (Luke 20:22–25)

The crowd consisted by and large of people who embraced the notions of Genesis, who believed the whole world to be made by God and in God's image, and who understood themselves to be children of God. They got the point, even if it left them unsettled, as the text indicates. Only the little coin bearing the emperor's likeness, stamped with his image, could be said to belong to the emperor. All else is God's.

What does it mean to be created in the image of God? Like any detective searching for a long lost parent, we take our clues from what we may discern and deduce from our own selves and experiences. Our search for God literally begins at home. What evidence do we have of God in and through those closest to us, those we trust most deeply?

This question raises an important issue—the weight of relationship and experience in our perceptions, and distortions, of God. Before we attempt to answer the question itself, we need to consider the limitations of what we can know in any relationship, but especially in our relationship with God. If we derive insights into God in and through our most intimate relationships, then within those same relationships we are exposed to false, even dangerous, notions of God.

The modern feminist critique of a male-dominated Christianity deserves to be heard and heeded. Perceptions of God modeled in a particular maleness are incomplete at best and, at worst, patently blasphemous. The second commandment, forbidding graven images of God, extends beyond sculptural figuration; any image of God—any imaginary conception of God—holds the potential for idolatry and is thus condemned by this tenet. The authors of the commandment may not have foreseen photography or film or digital imaging, but their prohibition extends deep into the human capacity for imagining, and for rendering that imagination tangible in media.

The power and potential of human imagination to project our experience of one person onto another is a phenomenon well known to any counselor. A child bullied or brutalized by any adult, especially a parent, will long afterwards find it difficult to trust. An abusive mother or sister can forever scar one's relationships with women; an abusive father or brother may long afterwards distort or damage one's relationships with men.

The same holds for the power of human experience to shape our image of and relationship with God. A culture dominated by men, at the expense of women and children, whose domination extends to an exclusively male image of God, shapes the social and individual imagination of God. Even our Hebrew ancestors knew and appreciated the power of such influence. In reading their accounts in scripture, we see that their image of God is formed of their experience of authority. God is called *lord*. Subsequent generations down to our own retained this word and its corollary, *king*.

What did our ancestors mean when they described God in such tangible, political terms? At base, all they meant was that God was for them the ultimate authority. God was also, eventually, called *father*—in part, perhaps, because God was perceived to be the ultimate source, creator, and author of all things. But to see what our ancestors in faith meant, and how those meanings evolved, one has to read their narratives deeply and sequentially. In so doing, one discerns the subtle twists and changes that emerge from a living relationship.

A child's experience and perception of parents are similarly dynamic. The innocent dependence of the infant, especially toward the mother, is seemingly indiscriminate, a purely loyal attachment of animal instinct between a new life and its physical source. This gradually gives way to the growing autonomy of the child, whose emergent independence tests boundaries, and trust, in bold challenges and brash, even cruel, outbursts—"I hate you!" and "You never loved me!"—seeking only affirmation. Just as one might "spring" on a suspect board prior to stepping out and trusting it with one's full weight, such challenges are a way of testing the strength of a relationship.

In adulthood, the mature person sees the parent quite differently. While no human relationship is fully secure from damage or hurt, in the best of circumstances the adult emerges safely into full selfhood with appreciation for the difficult business of shepherding (another image our ancestors held of God) that parenting is. For many this is when the cycle begins anew, as the role of parent is bestowed upon the newly formed adult.

This progressive understanding of God is well documented in the scriptural narratives. But it isn't neat and tidy, or always apparent. It is every bit as complex as our experience of human family and relationship. To return to the prior metaphor of the elephant, much depends upon which part one has hold of, and when. Two children of the same parent, growing up a decade apart, experience the same parent in quite different ways. The first child encounters the tentative insecurity of a new parent, unsure of how to relate to the baby or to care for it. The later child knows a seasoned child-rearer of deeper and more extensive experience, with greater confidence. Or perhaps the first child knows only a parent captive to addiction, while the later child knows a parent several years into recovery. Or maybe the first child knows parents struggling for financial necessities, while the later child experiences parents comfortable with their assets, or just the opposite—the first child born in security and the later one in poverty.

In our imagining of God, we are not to be dissuaded from such creative envisioning. What we are to avoid is any fixation. If God is more than any of us can imagine, more than all of us together can imagine, then whatever we imagine of God will always be partial and temporary. Why, then, should we imagine God at all?

We can and should imagine God because in the act of imagining, we admit God into ourselves and invite God into the realm of our own experience. Our imagining is itself a profoundly spiritual discipline and religious devotion. Our imagining God is our deepest and most important encounter with God, deeper even than prayer. Or I should say, deeper even than the way we usually conceive of and practice prayer. While we may tend to approach prayer as a monologue, the traditional understandings of prayer are conversational and demand attentive listening. Admitting God to our innermost reflective self, entertaining God in imagination, invites God to the center of our attention, where we can listen most intently, hear and perceive most lucidly.

For good or ill, as Twain's quip maintains, we do imagine God in our own image. But in imagining God, and allowing God full access to our imaginative, creative self, we invite God to shape us in God's image. The danger of conversation—and every living, intimate relationship is a conversation—is that in genuine conversation we expose ourselves to the possibility of change. Engagement with another carries the risk of transformation.

We see an example of this transformative power in Matthew 17:1–13, the story of the Transfiguration of Jesus. In that story, still somewhat early in his ministry but far enough along to pause for reflection and consider his next steps, Jesus withdraws quietly with three companions. Withdrawing further, apart from but within sight of his companions, Jesus is depicted in conversation with Elijah and Moses, perhaps searching the meaning of his life and vocation in conversation with his spiritual (and vocational) ancestors. In that interchange God is present, even depicted as such in the (imagined?) proclamation to the attendant disciples, Peter, James, and John, "This is my Son . . . ," and mediated through the ancients, Elijah and Moses.

Whatever his state of mind and heart at the outset of the retreat, Jesus is clearly changed by the imaginative conversation. He is so changed the difference is apparent to his companions, who describe him as "transfigured," completely altered in appearance. At the very least, an uncertain and unsure Jesus, seeking insight into his life's meaning and his ministry's purpose, in conversation has been significantly changed, encouraged—literally given heart—and emboldened with such clarity of meaning and resolution of purpose that he is literally aglow. It's a powerful story of change and the transformative power of imaginative engagement with God.

The powerful forces of relationship are both good news and bad. Change does not come easily, and involuntary change is one of our deepest fears. The fear of vulnerability to change beyond our own control is an impediment to conversation, to relationship. This fear isolates us, and leads us to the next question of the catechism: Why do we live apart from God and out of harmony with creation?

Why do we experience, even in the very lap of comfort, a profound loneliness? Why do personal accomplishments and material possessions fail to satisfy our hunger? Why, in even the closest and most loving relationship, do we know estrangement? And the most painfully perplexing corollary: Why don't even the best and most holy acts protect a person from danger, hurt, and death?

The simple answer to these questions is freedom. As the suffix *-dom* (meaning office, realm, or state, as in dukedom, kingdom) suggests, freedom is a state, a realm. It is the place or state of apartness — of not being tied, secured, or otherwise bound. Freedom is both positive and negative. I enjoy my freedom, my liberty to experience my own life apart from obligation, expectation, or judgment. At one extreme, this is the attractive (at least to me) side of freedom. But the other extreme is that in freedom I am cut loose, adrift and resident in a place populated only by me. Freedom is my heart's fondest desire, and my worst nightmare. Can't live with it, can't live without it.

Our ancestors evidently believed that God not only made everything, but that God's creative activity was a completed action; having come to the end of the sixth day, God declared all that had been made to be good, and God rested on the seventh day. That is to say, God set the created order free as an artist completes a work and thereafter tampers with it no more. The work of art is what it is. Such an understanding of the world, and of God's creative activity, is consistent with a God whose own name is "I am."

Freedom is an inherent quality of God's creation. Remembering that faith is always a matter of trust, not surety, if the world and all therein truly are the creation of God, and if life is, indeed, a gift, then freedom is a condition of both creation and gift. The artist completes a work, offers it as gift to others. Once finished, the work is beyond the artist's control. Once given, a gift is beyond the giver's control. The person apprehending the work of art or receiving the gift is free to interpret the art or use the gift in whatever fashion, without regard to the artist's intent or the giver's expectation.

But a work of art is inert, impassive. While a piece of art can inspire, can even be said to have a "life," it is not a living creature, does not bear responsibility for itself, cannot recreate itself. It does not act, but is acted upon. Deists, among whom we may count Thomas Jefferson and George Washington, imagined God as a divine watchmaker who, having made this marvelous, complex world and everything in it, set the spring and left it free to run. But this notion is not wholly satisfying, is as deficient as the art/gift analogy. If, as an old saying puts it, analogy is like a dog walking on three legs, here the pup tips over.

Freedom, in creation, consists of more than simply being completed, set apart, whole. Therefore, our ancestors spoke of God's creative activity as analogous to human birth. God's creative act is not as much like artist or giver as like parent. Both Hebrew and Christian scriptures speak of God's begetting, God's nurturing, of creation's difficult delivery. Within relationship, freedom is tempered by family.

Love demands freedom, cannot exist without it. If we believe that God was motivated by pure love to create us, if we believe that God created us for love—in order that God might love and be loved—then freedom is a condition of that creation. For love is untethered. Pure love is unconditional. As Andrew Greeley once wrote of friendship, in any truly loving relationship each person in the relationship is and must always be free to turn and walk away, but chooses to stay.

My father loves me, my mother loves me, and I love them. Each of us longs to be loved, but none of us wants to be loved simply *because* we are tied by blood, by birth. I don't want to be loved out of duty or obligation. I want to be loved for who I am, for what I am, apart from any necessity. The painful struggle of every person to find and experience such love demands that we be severed from all other ties, that we live in that realm called freedom, which is lonely and apart.

One of the marvelous, and to many eyes hidden, qualities of Hebrew scripture is the way it relates Israel's relationship with God, and God's relationship with Israel, as analogous to human growth and maturation. In the long story spanning generations and books, one encounters a God who, like any human parent, brings life into being and then must struggle to let that life be. The story is filled and fraught with pathos and humor on both sides. At times, Israel is happily surprised to be allowed so much rein and alternately dismayed to feel so abandoned. Elsewhere, God seems genuinely taken unawares by Israel's rebellion and yet deeply moved by Israel's painful falls. These are the consequences of freedom and choice, the consequences of love.

I remember being awakened by an early-morning telephone call some years ago. As I emerged from the depths of sleep I heard my youngest sister's tear-filled voice on the other end of the line. A much-loved aunt had died, a woman dear to us all, but especially to my sister. It was my sister's first close encounter with profound loss. The deceased aunt's daughter, our cousin, was of my sister's age. Reared within the tight bounds of rural family life, under circumstances rapidly fading from our modern experience of family, these two young women shared much in common. They were, in many ways, the younger image of their mothers—sisters whose lives were bound by common experience, and by the shared experience of painful terminal illness, now ended in death.

My sister's grief poured out, filling the wires that spanned the distance from the acreage in piedmont North Carolina cleared by our grandparents to Lake Michigan's shore in Chicago, and finally reaching the question I knew would come. Why? Not why the death, why the loss? But why the pain, why this unassuageable hurt? My only answer then or now: this is the price of love. To comprehend this costliness is essential to engaging the subsequent question posed by the catechism: Why do we not use our freedom as we should?

Why do we not use our freedom as we should? At one level we can argue that we do not use our freedom as we should because of ego, an innate selfishness. It does seem that we are naturally inclined, even genetically programmed, to pursue personal gain. Far beyond a Darwinian survivalism, we seem compelled to persist against all odds, to resist anyone and anything that might impede our own succession to ultimate power.

These proclivities have been with us for some time, long before power lunches and power ties, before road rage and the rudeness of entitlement we experience all around us. Our inner tyrant, like our inner child, seems to have been known as far back as Genesis.

I love the mythic story of Adam and Eve, in part, because it seems, like a much-loved movie, to reward each new encounter with a new insight, a different perspective. In this respect it bears much in common with the parable, a story that invites interpretation based in experience, yielding different meaning to different hearers.

Adam and Eve, as we find them in the garden, are the very model of all we aspire to be. They have no hunger, no labor, stimulating surroundings, meaningful activity, complementary companionship, a comfortable home, and boundless liberty. They are, by all our material standards, the picture of fulfillment. There is only one condition upon their life: they are to be satisfied with what they are and have.

Within Eden there stand two trees, the Tree of Knowledge and the Tree of Eternal Life. Presumably, Adam and Eve are free, even encouraged, to tend and enjoy each of these trees, as they do all the other creatures of the garden. But the harvest of these trees belongs not to them, but to God. Like the analogical shepherd of later stories, they are to be stewards of the trees but not owners. The owner does not tell them they shall never taste the fruit of the trees or share the harvest, only that they are not to presume to eat the fruit before it is given.

They are like children at Christmas, obsessed with what's under the tree—or in this case, what's *in* the tree. The story lays blame upon the snake (if only to explain why, of all earthbound creatures, this one was denied legs); their obsession needed no outside impetus. They are convinced in themselves that the possibility of some future experience of the fruit is insufficient. They want not just to taste the fruit, but to devour what the fruit has come to stand for—the owner of the tree. They eat. And the rest is, literally, history; the result of their action is the introduction into human experience of time and all its consequence.

This very sophisticated story is not the end but the beginning of an understanding of who and how God is, of who and how we are, and how we became not only children of God but creatures of time. Clearly, the story indicates, the choice was ours. That means, among other things, that any and every consequence of this choice is our responsibility. This is an important consideration whenever exploring the age-old quandary of why and how evil is introduced into and became operative in this realm bounded by time. If, as the story suggests, all human suffering results from the confinement of time bounded by birth at the one extreme and death at the other, this is a pivotal point.

Why would we make such a choice? Why do we live with these consequences attributed to ancient ancestors? Why aren't we given opportunity to choose for ourselves? All good questions. But these are all questions presuming that the story is one of historical realities. If we accept that the story of Adam and Eve, and subsequent stories expanding upon it—stories like Dante's *Inferno*, the anonymously authored medieval mystery and miracle plays, and Milton's *Paradise Lost*—are etiological fables, stories that examine the world as it is known and experienced and seek to explain how this world came to be, we appreciate all the more the wisdom and insights these stories impart. Furthermore, when we examine these stories thoughtfully, we find that in every instance, these tales do not purport to explain the world as we know it as wholly God's doing, but rather as *our* doing, as a collaboration, the fruit of relationship in freedom. God's intentions, as these stories maintain, are for good. Chief among those "goods" is the gift of liberty and the invitation to co-creativity. These are what any parent wants for a child; we desire that our children be free to grow into their own gifts and abilities, and that they use those gifts in ways that bring happiness and fulfillment to their own lives and to the world around them.

But the gift of freedom entails risk. In the early years of a child's life, we restrict freedom for the sake of the child and the world. Telling the toddler never to leave the yard not only preserves the toddler's life, it safeguards the happiness and fulfillment of every driver who might accidentally injure or kill that child. As the child grows, and our trust in the child and in the efficacy of our instruction and guidance increases, we extend more freedom to the child. In extending more freedom, we are also extending more responsibility.

When the child errs and mayhem results, we assess the experience. Was our instruction incomplete, our permission premature? Was the child deliberately testing us or our instruction? Who's to blame? Usually, all to some degree.

The Bible contains many fables and parables about this process as it pertains to our experience of God. One of my own favorites is the tale of Noah and the Ark (Genesis 5–9). I like this story because it comes to us from earlier stories told long before our Hebrew ancestors adopted and adapted it to their own use. I am especially fond of it in the biblical telling because in the end, God accepts responsibility for a misjudgment and misbehavior.

As the story goes, God's people are misbehaving and God, like any parent pushed to the limit, gets angry. God's anger mounts, but God is conflicted; while God wants to punish, God doesn't want to destroy completely what's been created. God just wants to start over. So God chooses the best parts of creation and sets them aside, like a sourdough starter, encouraging Noah to build an ark and fill it with one pair of every creature. Then comes the flood, destroying everything. Forty days and forty nights of rain. In a later story, recorded in the book of the Exodus, seeking to start over with Israel, God sends them on a long journey for forty years. Why forty years? Probably because to get a clean start, a whole generation needs to die and its memory erased; we all know the hampering effect of "but we've always done it this way." But that's another story.

So the waters come and the waters go, leaving the ark and everything in it high and dry. Then comes the remarkable part of the story: the rainbow. The world isn't the only thing changed by the waters; God too is chastened by the flood. God sees the destructive power of anger and makes a promise never again to unleash this power against the creation. The rainbow is created, this phenomenon that can only appear when it rains. The rainbow will be a sign, not just for humans, but for God. That humans—who certainly would have given pause every time a sprinkle fell from the sky—may derive comfort from this visible reminder, is only part of its purpose; the rainbow is placed in the heavens primarily for God's sake, to remind God never again to let anger stand between God and the creation.

Evidently creation is as much a learning experience for God as for us. Why should this seem so strange? Does it diminish God to suggest that omniscience may be a limited knowledge, or at least a knowledge acquired progressively? It is true of human experience that one may be brilliantly endowed with intellectual knowledge, *scientia*, and be painfully bereft of relational experience. Or perhaps the fault is in our own interpretation of omniscience, which is first defined as "having infinite awareness, understanding, insight" (Webster) and only secondarily as "possessed of universal or complete knowledge." Is not a limitless awareness and capacity for understanding more consistent with our experience of God's grace than an encyclopedic grasp of fact?

Yet there is a more compelling possibility to the notion that God may be "surprised" by us. Is it not possible that God created all things for the sheer pleasure of relationship, for the dynamic process of loving that comes of love's unpredictability, even its irrationality? So much Christian theology has denied God this dynamism by confining God to a prison of knowledge. As is often asked, what matter is it that God knows everything if God cannot intervene to prevent tragedy or destruction? The matters of God's foreknowledge and its correlative, predestination, are critical facets of some Christian theologies, including Anglicanism. But it bears repeating that theology is itself an activity and expression of faith, not fact. The God I encounter in scripture, and love dearly in experience, is a God who can delight in surprise, and can sometimes fall prey to it.

The element of surprise in relationship has both positive and negative dimensions. We can be pleasantly surprised. In such moments, we are moved to a keener experience of joy, pleasure, and satisfaction, or the host of other delights that life and love offer. We can also be taken by surprise, momentarily plunged into fear. In these moments, we are prone to experience and express the darkest responses imaginable. Caught unawares, seized by fear, we may become enraged, lashing out verbally or physically with all the force we possess, and more. Enhanced by adrenaline, our force can move us to kill.

The tale of Noah, and a godly anger sufficient to drown a world, is not so difficult for me to understand. My genetic pool includes a generous helping of Mediterranean temper—the short-fused, easy-to-ignite, slow-to-forgive type. When I was eighteen years old, I engaged both my parents in argument. The cause or subject of the disagreement has been long forgotten; besides, at eighteen one needs little or no provocation to pick a fight with parental authority. In the course of the fray, I made a hateful remark to my mother. Unfortunately, I was standing perilously close to my father at the time. In a split second I felt the sting of his hand across my face as I heard him say, "Don't ever speak to your mother that way," and just as quickly felt my arm raise to a position poised to return the blow. We were all caught by surprise, and not the kind that delights. Though we continued the verbal fracas, it quickly de-escalated to a point where all could retreat with some semblance of embattled dignity intact.

Nothing was irreparably broken. My face was only reddened and only my pride had been wounded. Apologies healed almost everything that had been fractured. The most significant outcome, however, was our learnings. Each of us, my father and I especially, learned something about the depths of our own feelings, and the capabilities of our physical powers. My father apologized and never again raised a hand against me. I apologized, too. While we continued for years thereafter to disagree on various matters, some far more consequential than whatever engaged us that day, this experience tempered us. Our arguments were no less passionate, but we were challenged to work through them carefully—literally taking care not to be taken unawares by destructive surprise. This challenge led us eventually to new surprises, of the delightful kind, as we discovered that disagreement need not mean death and destruction.

My family's experience, like the experience shared by God and

Noah, brings us to the catechism's next question: "What help is there for us?"

To say, as the catechism does, that "Our help is in God" begs the question—until we sit with the question, and the response, for a while. This terse response offers no extensive explanation, no expansive argument. Instead, it invites us to brood. With the patient tenacity of the hen on her nest, we sit on this simple sentence. In the brooding, the patient attending, it may come to us, as it came to my father and me in our separate spaces—me behind the closed door of my room, him in the quiet of his study—that what we needed most to move beyond our fearful confrontation was already ours: we had each other. We were, in the most literal sense, "in" one another. We were father and son, united in a bond of kinship and creation.

We were also companions, a word that oddly means "with bread" (com and panis). While this word takes on a profound dimension in the context of Christian Eucharist, it is a central image in my family. The one place where we were all united was at table, a place my father and mother insisted we occupy at least once a week throughout our lives in their household. Across generations and cultures, the practice of eating together has defined intimate relationship. Once admitted to the table, one is outsider no more, but embraced by the bonds of the shared meal.

I in my room and my father in his den would eventually need to eat and, when we did, we would share the same table. Our separation, though necessary in the moment, was not forever. The fact of our kinship and the reality of our having to come to table also challenged us to come to terms with each other, with our enmity and its reconciliation. The proximity of relationship that had allowed us to risk hurting each other physically was also the mechanism by which we might be healed. But one of us would be challenged to take the lead.

Thus we come to the question: "How did God first help us?" Once again, I find the story of Noah instructive and insightful.

One of the strangest aspects of Noah's story is that nowhere in the tale does any human offer apology for whatever it was that precipitated the flood. All responsibility falls upon God. It is God who is sorry for having made the world in general and humans in particular (Genesis 6:7). After the flood, it is God who does all the talking, expressing a renewed commitment to the whole creative enterprise (Genesis 8:21ff.). God seems to understand that the world, and humans, are the way they are because of God's choice to endow creation with freedom. That the outcome has proven a disappointment to God is not entirely the world's fault.

In this story God learns that love carries consequence. The cost of freely given love is risk, the fruits of which may be painful, or glorious. God is challenged, and chastened, by the experience with Noah. If God is to continue in relationship with the creation, reconciliation must be effected. God, being the literal elder, the progenitor, in this relationship, makes the first move. The origin of symbolic peace is traced to this story in which God extends to Noah an olive leaf in the beak of a dove.

It was my father who first offered apology after our altercation. Who's to say whose place it was to make the first move? Perhaps my father understood that as progenitor, as the more authoritative in years and power, it was his responsibility to lead us both to a new, renewed relationship. How did he come to this knowledge, much less to act upon it? Why he acted as he did is a mystery to us both. It neither needs nor demands explanation. Whether I encounter it in the story of Noah or in the text of my own life, it is wisdom. Which is to say, it is knowledge born of experience of love in relationship.

This experience in my own life, and this written narrative of it, reveal the role and realm of companionship in the life of faith. As you read it, you gain greater understanding of me and my father—you know us, to some extent. In the same way, I know Noah and even God as both are perceived through the eyes and experiences of those who created, treasured, and transmitted those stories to us.

As my nieces and nephews read my story, as I trust some of them one day will, they'll better understand their uncle and their grandfather. They will know something of the pain and struggle that forged the love of our family. When they encounter similar struggles in their own families, as they no doubt will, they will know the experiential connection they share with others in our family. Reading this story on these pages, seeing this story placed side by side with one from the Bible, familiar from Sunday School, they may understand their own experiences as common to humankind itself.

In such ways our companionship is extended. We share the table, derive our life and nurture from an expansive family. We are united through time to our earliest ancestors. We share a common history in our common origin in the One who has made us who we are and given us all that we have. We are united to God and to one another in an unbreakable bond of love. We are inheritors and authors of a literature including but not limited to the Bible. Our stories, all of them combined, comprise the longest, richest tale of love—a work in progress that reaches back to a time before alphabets, extends into this moment, and stretches beyond sight into a realm beyond death itself.

This is the text of faith. It is more than the sixty-six books of ancient writings that make up our Bible, even if that be the touchstone by which we take meaning's measure. It is our story, *your* story, the text of life itself, whether written on paper, or shared in talk, or carried in the heart. This is our inheritance and our legacy, a trove of wisdom accrued as only wisdom can be—through experience encountered, pondered, and shared.

It is with this wisdom that we come to the next portion of the catechism, in which we explore the accumulated perspectives of God, the world, and humanity that shape and guide our relationships with each other.

2

Traces of God

EFORE THE CATECHISM engages issues of how we might use our freedom, how we ought to behave, it explores the essential prerequisite of what we believe of our own being and God's. In other words, we begin with what *is* before proceeding to what ought to be. Having begun with some of the issues pertaining to what it means to be human, we turn to the being of God.

From the earliest considerations of godhood there have been those who eschew any attempt to conceive of God as possessing human characteristics. The limitations of human thought, perception, and language demand that we begin any discussion of God with the disclaimer that whatever we may think or say of God can only be partial. However, that limitation need not prohibit or deter every attempt. Indeed, the partiality of human perspectives only underscores the communal nature of faith; because neither I nor you can comprehend the totality of God, we depend upon one another to gain whatever we can know of God.

Unfortunately, human nature and institutions being what they are, we are less inclined to cooperation than to competition. The powers of knowledge, suspicion, and jealousy conspire to encourage us toward claims of God framed in terms of either/or. We tend toward the attitude that God is either as I conceive of God, or as you conceive of God—that our different perspectives of God are mutually exclusive. The biblical story of the Tower of Babel (Genesis 11) and its symmetrical counterpart, the story of Pentecost (Acts 2), point to the dangers of exclusive views of God and encourage us toward a mutuality that understands God to be both/and—that our different perspectives enlarge our perspective of God. God is both what I perceive of God and what you perceive of God, and more. Those who truly seek a deeper knowledge of and faith in God face an inexhaustible wealth of human perspectives of God as numerous as the peoples who inhabit the earth, reaching back through the vast realms of recorded history and beyond.

The story of Babel recounts the legend of human diversity. How did it happen that a people descended from one couple, Adam and Eve, became many peoples? As the tale puts it, when all the peoples of the earth were of the same tribe—all one people—they set about to build a vast city and a tower reaching toward heaven. Some have perceived the tower as an attempt to reach the throne of God, though the story omits this understanding. Read quite simply, it is a tale of human exclusivity and the tendency to use human talent, skill, and ingenuity to bolster our independence and security. "Let us make a name for ourselves," the proposers of the project declare. "Otherwise," they fear, "we shall be scattered abroad upon the face of the whole earth." The instinct to cocoon, to build high the walls, dig deep the moat, and raise up the drawbridge—whatever images one associates with insularity, with fortification against the challenges of dispersion, diversity, and change—motivated their construction.

But God is perceived as displeased with this project. It does not accord with God's intent for humanity. Comfortable as home is, secure as hearth may be, God's creatures are made and called to live in the world, not just a walled-up corner of it. Furthermore, they are intended for communal interdependency, not exclusive insularity. So

God "refines" the creation with the introduction of multiple languages, a device that enhances difference and offers possibility for new life.

Of course, like all gifts, the gift of diverse language brings potential for good and ill. With the possibility of new life comes also the threat of conflict and death. Multiple languages and cultures offer an enlarged experience and perspective, but they also offer fragmented exclusivities and tribal rivalries. The Pentecost story recalls the issues of diversity raised in the story of Babel. While it does not mention Babel by name, the significance of language in the Acts account would have been obvious (and still is) to anyone familiar with the earlier tale. At Pentecost God's original intent is rearticulated in the experience of those in the story. Caught up in an outpouring of enthusiasm, a babble of many people speaking at once and each in a different language, they are suddenly seized with the insight that though they are speaking in different tongues, they are proclaiming a common reality—each is witnessing to the remarkable acts of God in their own lives.

Thus as we come to the image of God as father, an image of God fraught with controversy, we begin with the understanding that this image, like all images of God, is only partial. It is also an image that has been central to the community's perception of God for many centuries. To reject this or any other image out of hand is to do violence to a tradition and discard a perspective as valuable as any other. As the apostle Paul urged in a different time but in circumstances similar to modern debates over the image of God as father, even perspectives deemed weak in the eyes of some deserve inclusion and respect in the body of Christ which is the church (1 Corinthians 12). That being said, what wisdom may be perceived in the notion that God is like a father?

Despite the limitations the image holds for many people today, there is a wisdom in the ancient perspective that God possesses attributes common to the male gender and fatherhood. Quite apart from the complex behaviors of human fathers that range from benign kindliness to active brutality, all fathers share one biological commonality: paternity is a matter of faith. Or it was before the advent of DNA testing.

One's relationship to God is premised upon faith, not empirical scientific knowledge. Until scientific DNA testing made paternity verifiable, a child's paternity was a matter of faith. Maternity could, even in ancient times, be verified. Any number of witnesses could attest to which child issued from whose womb. But even a woman of declared and devout chastity was not above suspicion; remember, Joseph was angry and embarrassed over the matter of Jesus' paternity. While a woman could be certain of her sexual partners, even that truth depended upon her testimony, which was never above challenge. Whatever else may have been derived from the notion of the fatherhood of God, this very essential point is itself sufficient to respect and ponder the reality it sought to convey.

The fatherhood of God, however, is not the only image or understanding given us by scripture. Indeed, it is only a minor and somewhat late perception, appearing more often in Christian scripture and later writings than in Hebrew scripture. The central image of God in the Hebrew texts is that of Creator.

Sexual congress is remarkably absent from Hebrew notions of God—possibly because other religions had monopolized sex as a basic theological theme. A nomadic people surrounded by host (and hostile) cultures whose gods were perceived in naturalistic terms and enterprises, the Hebrews were familiar with a host of foreign gods who cavorted and copulated—and encouraged their adherents to do the same—for the fertility and fecundity of fields and families. Their God, the God of Israel, was distinctive, different.

Their God was certainly about fertility, but their God was about that and more. Their God did not merely manipulate the natural forces of seed and harvest. Their God created. From nothing, before time itself, their God called everything forth. Their God was the genesis, the beginning, the substance and purpose, the meaning and end of everything. And not just of what could be seen and measured and known, but of everything beyond sight and science.

Yes, at one level, Israel's conception of God was one up on the competition. Theirs was certainly the ace in a deck of gods with many faces and houses even in the limited territories of their own sojourning. But while the motivations of human theology are often less than lofty, it was more than that. Any student of Hebrew scripture and its context knows that even the Hebrew perspective of God is a synthesis drawn from many sources. The stories of Genesis alone have their antecedents in tales found in other, earlier religions in the territories occupied by and surrounding Israel. Nor is monotheism the exclusive province of Israel; the Egyptians (among whom the Israelites lived as slaves) had conceived a monotheistic theology earlier.

Israel, however, represents a breakthrough in human understanding of God. One could, and probably should on principle, argue that the Hebrew understanding of God represents a significant communal theology. It is a perspective upon God that literally depends upon earlier perspectives. It does not dispute those perspectives, but includes, honors, and advances them by weaving them into a richer understanding of God. The God of Israel is not simply competitively superior to other gods. Though there are stories of such competition in the Hebrew narrative, as one would expect of any record of a people's political life, the overwhelming picture of Israel's God is of a God who encompasses the virtues of all gods and more. Israel's God is more expansive than exclusive.

Even Israel's understanding of its own particularity—its role as God's chosen people—is not perceived as exclusivity but as responsibility. The status of the chosen is not borne as a crown but as a duty, as an honor that brings obligation. Israel's particular responsibility—its particular response to its God—is to reveal that God to the world in such lovingly compelling ways that every nation will find refuge in their God. Thus, Israel's God is one who does not conquer but a God who embraces. Israel's God is capacious, a God who enlarges rather than diminishes life.

At the heart of this understanding of God is the image of the unitive Creator. God is the maker of us all, the One in whom everything finds its origin and its kinship. This is an idea so radical that even Israel could not readily or easily incorporate it into its life. It was a notion of God so advanced it could never be imposed; it could only be lived into. But it was central to Israel's life, and maintained its place at the center of Hebrew scripture as the common thread that weaves through every book included therein. God in everything, and everything in God. Essential oneness.

The institution, intuition, and implications of kinship in this unitive affirmation frame every aspect of the Hebrew religion and those religions derived from it. We inherit this legacy and continue to struggle with the challenges of living into it. It's a gradual and painful process, this living into a fundamental, essential kinship. Yet this is our call as believers in this tradition. This is also the central tenet that guides and frames our life: that we are radically united in common kinship with all creation as common creatures of a single creator God.

Moreover, we are invited into partnership with God who, we believe, enlists us as co-creators in the business of expanding this understanding of God's being and our being. Thus, as we draw closer to the issue of how we ought as humans to live within the freedom God gives us in life, we are encouraged to understand that any question of "ought" is predicated not just upon what we *do*, but begins in a fundamental understanding of who we *are*.

If we believe that we *are* related in a profoundly fundamental way to God and to all that God has made, then all our actions are informed by this essential relationship. Relationship provides a context within which we act. For better, and sometimes for worse, we act differently toward those to whom we feel close relationship. The intimacy of family tempers responses; we are more solicitous and polite, and more presumptive with and rude toward those with whom we share close relationship. But we understand that *because* we are related, we are fundamentally united in a common bond.

At its best that bond, and our commitment to it, encourages us toward actions of love and respect that support and preserve the unity. We understand, at some basic level, that our interest is bound up in the well-being of the other person. Well-being is an important component deserving a digression.

Acting upon well-being—our own or another's—is not the same as behaving to please. Modern psychology has taught us that there is a distinct difference between a healthy interdependence that seeks mutuality and a corrosive, even toxic, co-dependence that holds our own well-being hostage to myriad external forces and relationships beyond our control.

I believe my actions and yours can enhance or inhibit God's well-being. When, as a confessing believer in God, I seek to serve others lovingly and with respect, my doing so does more than "please" or appease God. When I act constructively, my life expressing commitment to the essential unity of God's creation, God is served. God's intent for me and for the created order is thus advanced in some small measure, and it may be that others are drawn into closer union with and commitment to God and God's purposes—all of which contribute to God's well-being. Of course, when I act otherwise my actions undermine God's well-being, contributing to disunity in every sphere touched by my actions and their repercussions. Neither God nor God's purposes for the creation are then served.

In other words, one is either working with God's intentions, or against them. In truth, we're always doing a bit of both since we proceed imperfectly, our knowledge and abilities insufficient to know always and everywhere what to do or how to do it. But creation is a dynamic and inexact business. Even God got a few surprises, as we have noted. Bringing something wholly unique, from nothingness, into being, as opposed to just crafting something from preexisting materials, entails the uncertainty of being itself. Creation is a process involving trial and error, joy and pain, success and failure.

To be engaged in this creative process with God, then, is to be part of an expansive, expanding enterprise in partnership with God. This is a different kind of relationship than that of worker to supervisor, master to slave. In a partnership the well-being of each partner and of the whole is the mission that informs every action, defines every decision, and serves as the standard for assessing health and wholeness. Engaging this process within the context of a unitive faith means that one is in partnership not only with God, but with everything and everyone God has made.

Within this unitive, integrated partnership we see ourselves as related to everyone and everything. From such a faith we derive our ethic and shape our morals. Our partnership commits us to a fundamental ecology. We do not act and are not made to "please" God or anyone else. Rather, we are created and called to participate in a unitive life, committed to sustaining and even advancing the well-being of the whole in and through every constituent part.

This is our creative challenge. The ways we respond to this call, the ways and means by which we contribute to this work of well-being, are our own creative exercises. While there are certainly established methods for sustaining well-being, we have not exhausted the ways to carry God's creative work forward. Every time we move beyond a stock response, risk a new improvement to the well-being of a person or any part of life on or among the planets, we create a new possibility.

New or radical as these notions may seem, I'm not making them up. While this is admittedly my own perspective, and one with which anyone can take issue, it is derivative. I cannot claim exclusive rights to these notions as my own creative property. I am deeply indebted to generations of believers before and contemporary with me whose perspectives have shaped and continue to influence my own vantage. In the following chapters I revisit some of them.

3

Promises, Promises

CLARITY OF LANGUAGE is an essential component of law, of theology, and of relationship. Previous generations of believers chose the word *covenant* to designate the nature of God's relationship with Israel, and with the Christian inheritors of that tradition. In modern usage and popular conception the barely perceptible differences between *covenant* and *contract* confuse the distinctive nature of God's relationship with us, and our relationship with God. The legal and economic dimensions of covenantal and contractual relationships are woven through centuries of religious understandings of this relationship. In both covenant and contract the key ingredient is the word *together*. In each type of agreement, those entering the covenant or contract set terms and conditions deemed mutually agreeable. The quality of the relationship is determined by subsequent behaviors. If either party in the agreement strays from the agreed terms, by either deficit or excess—meeting less or more of the demanded expectations—the other party is allowed redress. For example, if I fail to meet the terms of a contract to pay my mortgage in a specified amount by a specified date, the lender who has mutually agreed to these amounts and dates may sue me, not only to exact the due payment, but any interest lost by my negligence. Conversely, if I informally covenant to mow a neighbor's lawn for a specified fee on a specified date and decide to trim his shrubs, prune his trees, and weed his flower beds—exceeding the terms of the original agreement—he is under no obligation to pay me for these additional services.

These "economic" dimensions of contract and covenant, defining both benefit and liability, wind like the strands of a woven rope through the long history of theology. Questions of what God expects of us, and of what we expect of God, frame our understanding of our relationship with God. These dimensions are especially acute at times of crisis or trauma, giving rise to the perennial questions of why good people suffer bad things, questions that seek some explanation for tragic loss in the economy of our relationship. These dimensions also give rise to notions of preferential treatment or reward; when benefits exceed our expectation or are proportionally greater than our own performance merits, we count these as blessings, as signs of divine favor.

One of my favorite stories of the saints is attributed to Saint Theresa of Avila. She dreamed of meeting an angel. The angel carried a torch in one hand and a bucket of water in the other. "Why do you carry these things?" asked Theresa of her nocturnal apparition. "With the torch I shall burn all the palaces of heaven. With the bucket I shall quench all the flames of hell. Only then," said the angel, "shall we know who truly loves God."

The angel challenges the economic understanding of relationship with God based on punishment and reward. Sadly, this understanding prevails, buttressed by centuries of moral theology. Yet common sense tells us that when our most intimate relationships, relationships with spouse or partner, parent or child, reach this stage, they have deteriorated, even beyond repair. When such relationships devolve to the point of assessing benefit or deficit, when we maintain or sever our ties for fear of loss or for hope of gain, something has gone painfully wrong.

How, then, are we to understand our relationship with God? When I examine the scriptural record, I don't find much contractual language. What I do see is a God who makes promises. And promises are not quite the same as contracts or covenants. One distinct difference is that a promise can be, and usually is, unilateral. The word *promise* means, literally, "to send forth." Like the gift that it is, the promise is a free offer. It comes without condition.

When I make a promise I may wish for a certain outcome or a specific response, but I am not guaranteed either. When I make a promise to you, and you make a promise to me, each promise stands independent of the other; my promise to you does not depend upon your promise to me, or vice versa. I may fail at my promise without consequence to your promise. You may exceed your promise without consequence to mine. If a covenant consists of mutual promises (and I believe it does) then this is where covenant and contract part ways.

In the story of Noah we encounter the first occasion of divine promise. Our ancestors in faith who related that story perceived God as a promise maker. In the aftermath of the flood's destruction, God promises never again to destroy the creation with water. God makes the promise unconditionally. God does not say, so long as Noah and his kin abide by specific laws, I'll not cause the rains to come. No, God says never again. And as sign of that promise, and as a reminder to God, the rainbow is set in the sky, marking this resolve. This is unconditional gift, and unilateral promise. No matter Noah's subsequent actions, or his descendants' behaviors, the promise will stand.

The next time God is perceived as a promise maker is in the story of Abram and Sarai (Genesis 11ff.). The story of Abram and Sarai begins with a genealogy tracing Abram and Sarai's lineage to Shem, one of Noah's three sons. Functionally, the genealogy not only serves to establish the development of the Hebrew people from a specific family; it also serves rather like the old cinematic devices of swiftly moving clock hands, rapidly leafed pages of a calendar, or spinning newspaper headlines. It marks the passage of time. When the story picks up, we know we are many years removed from earlier events.

Abram and Sarai are the progenitors of Israel; they are the archetypal parents of a whole people. As such their stories are both personal and public, they tell the story of a whole people's relationship in terms of individual intimacy and particularity. In this sense they continue the etiological task of the authors of Genesis who, as you may recall, are recounting the story of how the people of God came to relationship with God. In the stories of Abram and Sarai emphasis is upon God's activity, God's promises. Abram and Sarai's own promises are more inferred than articulated, but they are clearly there.

The first promises God makes to Abram are of land and children. These gifts establish how Abram, whose people have been a nomadic tribe, came to inhabit a particular land, and how they secured that holding by force of population. It's easy to see how the economic dimensions of covenant are evidenced early. As their story continues, Abram and Sarai engage God in dialogue over the terms of these promises. They are getting older and still they have no offspring of their own to whom their land can be entrusted. In Abram's ninety-ninth year, a significant change comes.

Not only do the passage of ninety-nine years and the promise of a child to an aged couple signify the power of God's creativity, they also infer that the several covenants leading up to this crucial moment represent the give-and-take of mutual relationship. This long period is rather like a courtship and an engagement, and has many of the qualities of fledgling relationship. Hence the "economic" aspects of the relationship suggest the kind of testing that is prelude to all human trust. Interestingly (and tellingly) the several smaller covenants leading to the climactic moments of Genesis 17 do not hold the same importance as the ultimate exchange between God, Sarai, and Abram that establishes their covenant relationship.

This climactic exchange is marked, literally, by the human response to God's promises. While the narrative says that God mandated the changing of Abram's name to Abraham and Sarai's name to

Sarah, and specified male circumcision as signification of the promise, these are evidences of the human response to God, signs of some kind of promise made by Abram and Sarai.

The change of name signifies a change in relationship. Bestowing a child's name at baptism and the old tradition of bestowing a second, or middle, name at confirmation are tokens of particular relationship. The change of names that often accompanies marriage, and is manifest in the surname of a child born to the couple, signifies the relationships of husband and wife to each other, and of child to both. And after significant change in a person's life, it is sometimes the case that the person takes an entirely new name to mark that change, and entry into a new relationship with themselves and the world. Thus when Abram became Abraham, and Sarai became Sarah, the change of name signified for them, as well as for God, a new relationship.

What precipitated this change? What promise prompted this transformation? All subsequent generations agree that the essential promise of God is this: that "I, God, will be your God and you will be my people—forever." That's the promise. Pure and simple. And unilateral. There is nothing conditional in the promise itself. God promises to be our God and that we will always be God's people. Come hell or high water, literally.

And how shall we respond? With a reciprocal promise to embrace this relationship mutually, promising that God will be our God, and that we will be God's people. Abraham and Sarah embrace their new names. But names are ephemeral, mutable. So the pledge is made tangible in male circumcision. The removal of the foreskin is indelible. Even with our own sophisticated cosmetic surgeries, the act is practically irreversible. To mark the eternality of God's promise to us, and our promise to be God's people, the male body is irreversibly marked. No matter what may happen, no matter how he may violate the promise or refute it, his body will always give testimony to this essential relationship. In the most intimate and vulnerable part of his body, the male would always have evidence of the promise—not only the promise God had made, but as important, the promise the man had made. Like the rainbow God set in the sky as a reminder to God, circumcision was set in our bodies in token of our promise. That we may derive confidence from the rainbow, or that God might see evidence of our trust in a scar, are only secondary and incidental. The primary beneficiary of the sign in each case is the author of the promise.

Later generations have developed more subtle signets of promise, and not without controversy. The early Christian contention over the role of male circumcision as a sign of belief can be traced through the Acts of the Apostles and many of the apostolic epistles. The immutable character of physical marking is central to those arguments; for example, while many couples exchange rings as tokens of their promises, even resolving never to remove them from their fingers, such signs are impermanent. Yet, in truth, no sign of any kind is sufficient to hold us to our promise. Whether as drastic as bodily mutilation or as extravagant as adorning the finger with expensive jewelry, a living promise, like a living relationship, is a work in progress.

Because they are freighted by the weight of time and commerce, words like *contract* and *covenant* are insufficient to describe the nature of love in intimate relationships. Those who framed the story of the promise of God to Abraham and Sarah understood God to be the initiator of the relationship. This is consistent with the notion that all things find their origin in God. The human role is understood to be responsory.

What does it mean to be loved? What does it mean that God trusts me—that God loves me, has faith in me, entrusts me with hopes not only for my own well-being, but for the wholeness of all creation? How am I to greet such happy news? What does such good news mean for me?

Such good news is not always greeted with joy. Our own mistrust of ourselves, our own sense of unworthiness, our poverty of self-esteem can and sometimes do resist God's promise and protestations of love. Conversely, an overweening sense of our capabilities, our pride and overestimation of our self-worth can and sometimes do inhibit our reception of this love. Can one be said to have truly embraced God's love and its promise until one has come to a balanced appreciation of oneself?

Truly, the dynamic of living relationship is not stasis, but active balancing. Balance is always an energetic activity. We're always making myriad small adjustments just to remain upright in this world. In our relationships, we are seldom firmly in one place, but are always making adjustments. In some instances self-pride seizes the moment and we find it necessary to make apologetic correction, bringing a greater humility to bear. At other times, when sunk in a slump of self-pity, the reinforcement of encouragement can lift us back into balance. In our relationship with God, as in any other relationship, when the balances of mutuality shift, danger is in the offing. Thus we must not only be on guard for the human pride that presumes to know better than God, but we must also beware the self-abnegation that can make one the victim of an abusive deity. The God who promises and professes love for me does not tyrannize me. The God I have promised and professed to love will not capitulate to my manipulation.

One strives in healthy relationship for some equipoise. The best we can hope for is that, on balance, God's actions toward us and ours toward God will add up to the wholeness both God and we seek for ourselves and for the creation. To that end, we are never freed from the questions of love. We are always engaging, always seeking to answer what it means that God loves us, that we love God. For the believer these questions lead to evangelical and universal implications; as recipient of such love, to whom and with whom am I to share?

This struggle is at the heart of the stories of our Hebrew ancestors. They understood that one way to communicate a progressive love, a living relationship, was to chart that progress in a sequence of stories—many tales with numerous characters over many centuries. While we may learn from particular episodes, it's the whole story that chronicles the relationship at its heart, the relationship between God and the people. Our Hebrew ancestors understood that to be chosen of God, to be loved in particular by God, made them special. They were privileged, as anyone is privileged to be loved by anyone at any time. This privilege could, and sometimes did, lead to selfish notions of exclusivity. This is how sin manifests itself.

But this privilege also led to a sense of heightened responsibility. Love encourages, arouses a response. Love begets love. Generosity encourages generosity. Thus the gift of love elicits both question and opportunity: How shall I respond to such love? As the word *responsibility* suggests, our response is limited to our ability. How shall I respond to love, especially to God's love?

My response to God's love, my response to anyone's love, will be limited because I am limited. That is to say, my response to God's love, like God's love for me, will be particular, uniquely shaped to my own abilities. That's part of love's richness, that it is never duplicable. Love is never "matched," it is only multiplied. Part of the work of creation itself, love is as varied as any element of the whole. I can never give back either in measure or kind any of the love I receive.

As our ancestors came to this realization, they understood that the evangelical task of sharing God's love challenged them—called them—to a universal mission. God's particular love for them led them beyond their own narrow self-interest to embrace the whole of God's creation. As the poet Laurence Housman expresses it, "How shall we love thee, holy hidden Being / if we love not the world which thou has made?" (*The Hymnal 1982*, #573).

Israel, the successors of Abraham and Sarah, would wrestle for generations and bequeath to their heirs the question and the quest that remains to all who experience love: How shall I love in return?

4

Loving God

HOW SHALL I LOVE THEE? asked the poet. Let me count the ways. For our ancestors in faith, they numbered ten. Whether delivered on stone tablets on Sinai (Exodus 20) or evolved over centuries of living relationship with God, ten principles emerged as ways every human being is able to respond to God's love. As is often true in love, it is sometimes easier to define a loving response by the *via negativa*, literally by the negative way: if you really love me, at least you will not . . . . In this way we establish a minimum standard. Given that the positive potential of love is beyond our imagination, and beyond exhaustion, the ten commandments define the very least we can do.

Are they laws or learnings? If freedom is necessary to genuine love, and if God's love is freely offered, it seems inconsistent (if not antithetical) to dictate any standard as compulsory. The promise of God's love to Abraham and his successors, which precedes by several generations the episode at Sinai with Moses, is unconditional. As Israel lives into the relationship with God, and engages the question of how to love God in return, is it not possible that this struggle might lead the people to such principles? The process leading to this revelation is part of the gift of God's love, for without the love there would have been no struggle. So, as the story suggests, the principles do emanate from God, as part of the gift of God's love.

But are they conditional? Evidence suggests not. Consider that the tablets themselves are delivered into the hands of Moses, and conveyed to the people by him. Moses had himself committed murder; before God called him to lead the people of Israel, Moses had killed an Egyptian and fled in guilt (Exodus 2:11–15). Generations later, David, who would be anointed king over Israel, coveted Bathsheba, the wife of one of his soldiers; committed adultery with Bathsheba and arranged the murder of her husband, Uriah, by dispatching him to a certain death on the front lines of a vicious battle (2 Samuel 11). Despite these and other transgressions, God continued to love David, and his people. Obviously God's love was, as God's original promise indicated, both unconditional and eternal.

It helps to delve into the English word *commandment*. At base, the word means "to commit to one's charge." But the dictionary also points to the related word *commend* (to entrust), which also points to *mandate* (literally, to put or give—*datum*—into the hand—*manus*). Thus the word we have read as "law," with all the compulsion and consequence that word connotes, can also convey the measure of trust. The ten principles articulated in the Decalogue seem more learnings than legislation, not rules by which relationship is conditionally prescribed but the patterns by which we humans are able to respond lovingly to the God who loves us.

Thus the principles are divided into two categories: the first four principles describe the means by which we relate to God, the last six the means by which we relate to one another and the creation itself. All ten principles, however, offer a minimum standard by which we live out our love of God. They are the very least we can do.

My love for God begins in an acknowledgment of God's love for me. That may seem self-evident, but all love begins in the awareness of love's particularity. The very least I can do is neither to assume love nor take it for granted. All love, every love, is a gift. The Israelites' love for God began with the acknowledgment that the God who loved Israel, and this Israelite in particular, is the God who expresses that love in creating me and the world in which I live, the God who promised that love to me in Abraham, who reiterates that love in everything I have.

This acknowledgment recognizes not only the particularity of God's love for me, but the specificity of my God. My love for God entails my recognition of God's particularity. For our ancestors who lived among peoples who revered numerous gods by other names, this recognition identified Israel's God as distinctive. For us this principle is even more acute. To judge by appearances, it would seem that most of us who enjoy good health and moderate security in America ascribe such blessings to our own intellectual skill, hard work, and good luck. Our failure to attribute to God the love that we know is a profound failure in relationship. How then shall we love God?

The catechism and much of traditional Christian theology frame the question in the language of obligation: What is our duty to God? Unfortunately this approach only reinforces the economic notions of relationship and the contractual notions of relationship. Duty carries the weight of obligation, indebtedness. This framing of our relationship with God contradicts the freedom granted us by God. The relationship of debtor to creditor is not an apt analogy for a believer's relationship to God.

If life and love are God's gifts to us, given freely, they are extended with no expectation of repayment. Indeed, such an expectation would be unrealistic, as we lack the ability to reciprocate such generosity. God's love, covenant love, is promised to us by a God who is prepared to lose not only the interest but the principle itself. This is the nature of gift, and the nature of love. Love cannot compel reciprocity.

A gift's intended recipient is under no obligation even to accept. This is the painful reality of unrequited love. This is also why the Christian marriage service establishes at the outset the free consent of both partners. Even in places where the preliminary publication of the Banns of Marriage has dropped from common practice, a public declaration of consent remains in the marriage rite itself (*BCP*, p. 424). The prospective bride and groom are asked if they are freely and willingly undertaking the ritual that will culminate in the public proclamation of their covenant vows.

God's covenant with Israel, and God's covenant with each of us, lacks this preliminary. From the outset, God's covenant is unilateral: God professes love for the people and claims them for eternity. The matter of mutuality becomes the dynamic, and the defining characteristic, of faith. God grants me life, pledges me love, from eternity, for eternity. But I am neither constrained nor compelled by this pledge, for either would abrogate my freedom, would render the gift only a loan.

As our ancestors in faith gradually came to terms with this understanding of God, and God's covenant, they were at pains to avoid the economic equation but they were not always successful. Despite their best efforts, the matter of how we creatures might respond to God's love and promise tended to codification, solidifying into laws. This tendency toward stasis, or stability, is rooted deeply in human life. It's a response to life's dynamic.

Life is uncertain. That is life's excitement. That we cannot know, do not know, what the next moment will bring is what gives life its potency and vitality. This unpredictability is also inherent in love, and a living relationship. But the natural human instincts to self-preservation abhor this uncertainty. Our insecurity is in constant search of affirmation and assurance.

God's gift of life and promise of love ought to be—but seldom are—enough for us. We seek tangible assurance, proof. For this reason, religion—which is a human enterprise—tends toward material and emotional security, despite the reality that no religion can provide either. This is why religion is neither synonym nor substitute for faith.

Faith begins with an acceptance of God's gift and promise, but it only *begins* there. A living faith, like any living relationship, continues forever in the appropriation of and engagement with that gift and promise. In this relationship, there is mutual giving and receiving. Each party in the relationship—God and I, in this case—live daily with the uncertainties of life and love. Neither of us truly knows what may come next, yet each of us struggles to remain constant in love. Sometimes we laugh and rejoice together, other times we weep and wail together. Sometimes one of us is stronger, at other times the other is.

Do I really believe I am sometimes stronger than God? Yes, there are times when I feel keenly God's disappointment and pain. Who, loving God, can look upon the brutality one human can inflict upon another, and not feel the cosmic pain? Yet, there are rare moments when I am able to look upon such sin and still affirm that there is something within us all that is worthy of hope and love. Similarly, there are times in my own life when I despair, grieving deeply the pain of loss. But I am able to give vent to such deep hurt because I am confident that God sees also, and still finds even in my worst agony some cause for hope, something to love. This is faith's mutuality in living relationship.

Only within such mutuality am I, are we, free to embrace life fully. This is what I believe John means when his Jesus asserts, "I came that they may have life and have it abundantly," or as the New English Bible translates this familiar phrase, ". . . that [they] may have life in all its fulness" (John 10:10). This *is* life's fullness, a life embracing the full range of human experience and emotion. Without faith in God's loving companionship, without this mutuality of relationship, I not only would not know this fullness, I don't think I could endure it. It is too much for one person fully to comprehend and embrace, too much for one human being to survive.

It is for these reasons that I resist the legalistic and economic notions of the Decalogue and instead commend them as a guide to relationship, a relationship "how-to." They suggest to us how we might respond in kind to God's gift of life and pledge of love. Thus they begin with four points concerning our specific response to God. If I believe God freely gives me life and loves me eternally, what is such generosity "due"—what response represents a worthy human offering? Since I cannot truly reciprocate God's gift but can only respond out of my limited ability as a human creature, what can I give to signify my own commitment to life and love in God?

The first principle begins, "I am the Lord your God, who brought you out of bondage. You shall have no other gods but me." For our Hebrew ancestor, the first principle identifies God; the God who loves me is the God who delivered my people from bondage. My God is the God of creation, the God of Noah, the God of Abraham and Sarah, of Moses and his sister Miriam. The God who gives me life and pledges love to me is a particular God with an identity, and a history rooted in my own history. Thus I know who my God is, in part, because others before me have known this God and told me of this God. They have testified to this God's gift of life to them, and of God's pledge of love for them.

The catechism suggests that our response to this principle is to "love and obey God and to bring others to know [God]." *Obey* suggests a relationship of unequal power, of servant to master. But that may be the product of our own tendency to shirk the weight and possibility of mutuality. At its root, *obey* is a combination of the prefix *ob-*, meaning "toward," and the suffix *-oedire*—derived from the verb "to hear." The quaintly arcane biblical phrase "to incline one's ear" seems an accurate fit. To obey, then, means not to carry out orders, but rather to hear—to comprehend—the claim of God as origin of my life and the promise of God's eternal love of me.

This is a minimal response, yet it is what each lover desires of the beloved. When I profess my love for another person, I at least wish and hope to be heard; I desire that the other receive my affirmation even if they can do no more in response. This is simple acknowledgment, and the respect due any profession of love.

Bringing others to know God need not be the aggressive act it sounds. To know oneself to be loved is one thing; to confess oneself to be loved is another. I know my partner loves me. This is a matter not of simple empirical knowledge, but an act of faith ratified continually in our life together. I can and sometimes do keep that knowledge private. Yet, even when held in secret, this love in relationship informs and colors all other aspects of my life. In many instances, even those who know nothing of me may discern from my words and deeds that I believe wholeheartedly that I am loved.

More often, though, I confess that I know myself to be loved in particular, by one person in particular. That I can be loved says something about me, but says as much of the person who loves me. Such love suggests that I am a lovable person, perhaps even a trustworthy person, because someone else has deemed me worthy of love and trust. But even, perhaps especially, in my worst moments, that I am loved by another person says a great deal of that person: it evidences the tremendous grace and virtue of my partner that despite my worst faults, he still loves me.

It is true that in such moments, my partner may be deemed irrational. But love often *is* irrational. That's why believers have long maintained that faith is not necessarily a rational process, but neither is rationality all it's cracked up to be. We thank God, and our lucky stars, for love's irrationality.

One of my favorite fictional examples is a marvelous "Peanuts" comic strip that appeared, appropriately, on a Mother's Day some years ago. In that comic, Charles Schulz's little characters tell the story of a game of hearts played with Charlie Brown's mother. In the card game of hearts, the worst treachery one can afflict on an opponent is to engineer their receiving the Queen of Spades. In the particular game remembered, the children gleefully conspired to stick Charlie Brown's mother with the detested queen. What inspires their awe and marvel is her response. She receives the queen with grace, not a tantrum. And when the game ends in her defeat, she still bakes them cookies. To them, such love is irrational, falls outside the realm of the expected. And for that reason it is all the more notable, memorable.

When we confess ourselves to be loved, we acknowledge the gift in a public way. We need do no more than that to bring others to know God. Of course, we may boast of this love, in which case, we have already said something significant, and singularly reprehensible, about our self. But in any open confession of God's love of us, we are saying more about God than about ourselves. If God can love me, does love me, then God's capacity must be boundless. If there's room for me, surely others may be, are included. When I make this confession with such humility, I have gone beyond the minimum. When I actively encourage others to see, hear, and heed God's expansive compassion for them, I have gone the full distance.

Or have I? There's more to love than acknowledgment and even persuasion. My own insecurities never take a holiday. I am always susceptible to doubt. The grass always appears a bit greener elsewhere. When my security is at low ebb, the most profound protestations of love cannot satisfy. And when my security is at high tide, the confidence of love propels me to greed; if I can have the love of one person, why not more? Why not all?

These are the human tendencies that encourage us to idolatry. Thus the second principle is that "You shall not make for yourself any idol." Our ancestors wisely reasoned that if one takes God's gift of life and pledge of love to heart, it is enough. Now there's a word seldom heard: Enough. I'm usually afraid I won't have enough, or wishing I had more. Interestingly, the word *idol* means "phantom." An idol is a false representation, a pretender or impostor. It's not what it seems.

Therefore, anything other than a living relationship with God based in freedom and mutuality is an idol. This enlarges the definition of idol, but that may be more prudent than a reductionism that limits idolatry to the material. We are to put nothing in the place of God. Yes, that means we are not to make graven images, bow down to statues or emperors or money. But it also means that we are not to put position, power, prestige, or any other phantoms in place of God, either.

If I imagine God to be precisely or *only* as *I* imagine God, I have placed my imaginary deity in the place of the living God who gives me life and pledges eternal love to me. This is religious infatuation. It is to be in love with love, or worse, to be captive to the tyranny of my own affections. In human infatuation, one loses touch with reality and loves not a real person but only the imagined phantom of the other. In infatuation we do not allow the other to be a real person, but instead make the person a projection, a hologram, of all our neediness. No human being can fulfill such unfathomable expectation; God refuses to.

The God who gives me life and pledges love to me deserves to be loved only as God is, not as I might wish God to be. To put anything, especially my ideal, in God's place is to maintain that the God who loves me is not enough. My God is not perfect. My God, in a fit of pique, may have flooded the earth, as the story of Noah maintains. My God loves me, but my God also loves my enemies. My God created a world fraught with danger, gives me a life that includes a death. My God does not fulfill all my needs, else my God would not have given me the aid, love, and companionship of family, friends, partners. My God defies my notions of perfection. My God is. And if my God loves me as I am, not some unrealistic ideal of what I ought to be, then my God is due a comparable love. Anything else is idolatry.

"You shall not invoke with malice the Name of the Lord your God." That's the third principle, and a logical extension of true love. If I love God as God is, I cannot malign God for being God. I may not always like who God is, anymore than I always like who my parents are, who my partner is. Malice is an expression of anger, and anger is a response to fear, and fear is the opposite of faith.

That is a notable equation. When I speak maliciously of another person, my malice is often the response to fear of that person, which is a confession of lack of trust. Truly, that mistrust is sometimes justified. But wisdom compels me to look beneath my malice to recognize my fear and examine my trust. Is my mistrust justified? If so, then my testimony is not malicious, but truth; anyone or anything unworthy of trust deserves to be revealed for what it is.

But when my mistrust is unfounded, is based only on my fear of another's difference—whether it be a fundamental difference in perception of the world, or merely a difference of perspective—love and freedom demand my respect of that difference for what it is, and acknowledge my fear for what it is, which is to say that my fear is mine to own, and not a true reflection of who the other person is.

The catechism paraphrases this principle as showing "God respect in thought, word, and deed." This is an acknowledgment that our malice is not always expressed with grimaces and angry words, but in our subtle suspicions and in our postures of influence that lead others to distrust. At one level, this third principle is the darker expression of the second principle, against idolatry. If an idol is the projection of our unrealistic ideal, then our malice is the expression of our unfounded mistrust. And neither belongs in a loving relationship.

What does belong in a relationship? Time together. The fourth principle, "Remember the Sabbath Day and keep it holy," is as the catechism interprets it, a commitment to set aside regular time with God. Worship, prayer, and study are among the ways we pass this time.

Worship means nothing more or less than respect, worthiness. Here I'm afraid modern detractors of religion have a legitimate complaint. Much that passes for worship seems aimed less at expressing respect for God than it does at garnering the attention of appreciative spectators. Whether given over the excessive pageantry of high ritual or the casual ambiance of folksiness and talk-show ease, worship aimed at getting *our* attention has missed the mark.

If worship has an earthly analogue, it is probably the intimacy of the table. Which explains why most of the major religions of the world situate worship in a meal. Eating is a common, necessary act. It is also an awkward act. We eat seated, encumbered by a table and hedged about by others. Our backs are exposed, and so are our faces.

Our Hebrew ancestors understood the sacrality of our orifices. Eyes, ears, nose, mouth, vagina, urethra, anus are all points in the human body where the surface integrity of the skin is compromised by a vulnerable opening. The matters of ritual purity governing how one dealt with the emissions from and invasions into these openings were more than prudery; they were matters of life and death. What goes into our body and what comes out of it can have dire consequences for us and for others. Moreover, because these orifices are points of personal vulnerability, their functions are bounded by privacy.

Eating in public is a practice we take for granted. Yet for all our nonchalance, there is still something profoundly sad about a person eating alone in a public place. Like so many other sadnesses of public life, we have accustomed ourselves to looking beyond or away. But the momentary pang that hits when we do engage and fully comprehend the loneliness of the solitary diner only serves to remind what a profoundly vulnerable act eating is.

For these reasons, the table is a special place in any home. Whom we invite to share the table is a very personal matter. Family is usually welcome, even though particularly disruptive behaviors may not be. In my childhood, banishment from the table was a kind of hell. The embarrassment of being sent away, deprived of laughter and company, that deprivation only aggravated by the sharper awareness hunger brings, made this a painful discipline. It was usually my father who enforced this punishment, over my mother's protests. But his wise retort was always, "When they're hungry, they'll come back." He knew it wasn't just our physical hunger, but our hunger for inclusion, for society itself, that would compel us to reconsider, and repent, our disruption.

That same table was the site of some of my most important learning. It was a round table, a shape dictated by my father, who had grown up at a round table himself. And it was located in the center of the kitchen he designed and built for us. So I grew up at a table without a "head" or a "foot," located at the center of the meal's preparation, not removed from it. Until I left for college at age eighteen, I joined the rest of my family at that table for at least one meal each week. That, too, was my father's dictate.

What I might once have attributed to my father's heritage as a Sicilian-American son of immigrants, with all the male chauvinism that implies, I now appreciate as a discipline rooted in a much older tradition having little to do with gender identity and much to do with holiness itself. I do not mean the precious piety we associate with religion, but the rigorous practicality necessary to wholeness—from which the oldest notions of holiness are derived. Time at table as a family was a necessary discipline of the living relationship of family.

Moreover, from that discipline I learned to define family more broadly. Anyone who happened to "drop by" while we were at table would be invited to pull up a chair and share the table; the virtue of a round table is that it will usually embrace unexpected additions. Most importantly, that table did not maintain the same boundaries as the world.

When I was a teenager, a group of black students in Greensboro, North Carolina—just a few miles from that table in our kitchen—touched off a riot by sitting down at the lunch counter in Woolworth's. I did not understand. For years, Annabelle, my mother's black friend and coworker in the household chores, had shared our table. A few years later, estranged from the church of my youth and angry over its overt racism, I visited a local Episcopal Church. I carry the indelible memory of a black man and a white woman kneeling at communion, the chalice passing from his lips to hers without incident. It was, literally, a homecoming.

It was also a vision of God's realm. Maybe more than a vision. For Jesus maintained that in such moments, the kingdom, or realm, of God is very near. In such moments, the barriers of time and space—mortality—that spatially and temporally separate us from God are removed; it is on earth as we believe it be in heaven.

This is not to deny the potency or place of high drama in our lives. But we are reminded by the story of Christmas, of the nativity and incarnation, that we do not broach the barriers by mounting imagined replicas of God's realm on earth, but by risking our vulnerability. Impressive as they are, our cathedrals and temples have their ancestry in Babel's tower. God can and does dwell with us there, for there is no place where God is not. But God is also at every table, everywhere. Worship might then take on the best qualities of our dinner parties, and our dinner parties become occasions of profound worship. This is not heresy; this is holiness.

Similarly, prayer represents another way of spending time in relationship with a living God. Prayer, like worship, demands integrity. An analogy in human relationship is the communication, initiative, and mutuality necessary to a loving relationship.

It is essential to be clear in articulating our necessities and expectations in relationship; clairvoyance is not one of the gifts of blessedness. Most of us are quite adept at spelling out what we need, want, and expect. We're especially skilled at making these matters clear to God. Some of our most eloquent prose is devoted to this end. But if I never listened to others, I would soon be branded a bully, or ignored and avoided for the demanding boss I'd become.

Unfortunately, neither God nor we are completely coherent all the time. Listening is more than a passive reception of noise. Listening is a demanding discipline requiring rigorous practice if it is to become a genuine skill. Listening demands all our senses, and the gift that seems to distinguish us from other animals: reflection.

Thus in a loving partnership, one is constantly aware of need, and constantly responding. Most of the time, in love and of love, when we see something that needs our attention and care, we give it; we do not argue or quibble. Day in and day out myriad expressions of need flow to us, and their echoing responses of love and care flow out from us. Only when we are overwhelmed or otherwise incapacitated must we resort to a summit. Then we fight it out, or convene a conference, and negotiate. We grapple with our incapacities, and seek clarity so we can respond appropriately and move on.

If our prayer seems so much talking to ourselves, that may be an accurate perception. Nor is that necessarily bad. I'm a list maker; it's one way I talk to myself. I have many distractions in my daily life. I make note of those things I deem important lest I be distracted from them. I have many a mental conversation with myself as I engage the reflective practice of determining what each moment demands of me and how I might best respond.

Occasionally, I need time with colleagues to gain clarity on our shared goals and enterprises. Occasionally, I need time with God to gain clarity on our shared goals and enterprises. This is one kind of prayer. I think of it somewhat as the tip of a great iceberg of prayer, the greater bulk of which is unseen (and unheard), caught up, like me, in the currents of life.

That's why I value the Hebrew inclusion of study as a means of spending quality time with God. More than the ingestion of fact and literature, study is contemplation (literally, time and space set apart; *contemplation* shares a root with the word *temple*). It is the space within me that I open to others, where I admit their ideas, the reality of who they are. It is the place within me where engagement happens and from which change emanates. You may reach my heart, or my head, but these are only antechambers. Before you gain admission to my soul, before you are fully accepted into my life, integrated into who I am, we'll spend time in study. There we shall have our conversation, our give and take. That goes for God, too.

God neither demands nor deserves more than you do. God wishes only to share that time, come into that space, there to engage the conversation. There God is known to me and I am known to God. This is love's deepest expression. Thus we do not open that space wide or easily. Some of us never open it at all. We confine our relationships only to heart or head. Whether we live only in our heart or only in our head, or compartmentalize our relationships into one division or another, only those who engage us in study can be said to be integral to us. Only those who admit and engage others in study can claim integration as individuals, as members of society. For this reason, the Christian church has rightly maintained that one cannot truly be a Christian in isolation.

Wholeness of life, holiness in life, entails engagement with the fullness of life. Loving God engages us, involves us in life's fullness.

Loving God is not, of itself, enough. As Jesus maintained, one cannot claim to love God, and *not* love all that is *of* God, which is to say, everything else. It's all or nothing.

So the four principles guiding our love of God give rise to six more principles that emerged from our ancestors' experience and wisdom. What does it mean to live a life of integrity, a life whose every dimension is consistent with the love it claims to receive from God and the love it claims to have for God? How do we live in holiness, in wholeness, with our neighbors?

5

When Love
is Enough

IT IS A FAMILIAR SAYING that charity, a quaintly archaic word
for love, begins at home. When the principle axioms of the
faithful life turn to the matter of human relationship, they begin
with the most intimate arena, the family. Honor father and mother.

Honor, another word for respect, is not the equivalent of love.
Neither does it imply uncritical obedience or assent. Honor and respect connote an unequal relationship; honor and respect entail deference, and the person held in honor or respect is presumed to
possess authority. That authority may be the precedence of age and
experience, the responsibility of parenthood or office.

I can honor and respect the person who has assumed responsibility for my life and welfare even when we find ourselves in disagreement. The child knows this distinction and experiences it when
a parent's responsibility demands compliance to discipline. The citizen knows this distinction when compelled by law to comply with an
inconvenient or annoying demand established for the welfare of the
community.

But authority is the product of a delicate dialogue and a sometimes contentious debate. I must be convinced of the authority's sincere concern for my own welfare, individually and as part of the larger community. Moreover, the authority must merit this respect in constant and consistent fairness. For these reasons, the catechism paraphrases this principle: "love, honor, and help our parents and family; to honor those in authority, and to meet their just demands" (*BCP*, p. 848).

We know that parents can be abusive and authorities can be corrupt. Thus we are expected to hold them accountable. Accountability is a profound expression of love and respect. The sad experience of human dysfunction has taught us that blind deference to authority is not respect but complicity in systemic breakdown; we do not love or respect a person when we encourage and enable their destructive actions or attitudes. We accord dignity and express loving respect in demanding that each person live in wholeness and integrity, bearing responsibility.

We may learn this first in the household that encompasses our formation from birth to full maturity. We are formed for our lifelong vocation as humans by the families that surround us, by the communities that embrace us. It does, indeed, take a village to raise a child. Responsibility for every child's formation extends well beyond the intimate circle of blood kinship. As the interpreters of this catechetical principle suggest in their paraphrase, much hinges upon that phrase "just demands." Essential to each person's formation is the critical faculty of judgment, a foundational understanding and appropriation of justice. Without this core we risk being abusive and abused. Right behavior alone is insufficient. Life is too complex and creation too varied.

We encounter this problem in the frequent and simplistic appeal to "rights" as the justification for demands made upon the community. Justice—fairness—demands that we never use the word *rights* without its balance: *responsibility*. Indeed, the words can never truly be separated. Learning to weigh each in the balance is the work of justice, and equipping ourselves and each other to exercise this judgment is an essential task.

From this essential basis we move to the sixth principle, "You shall not murder" (Exodus 20:13). It is far too simple to read this tenet only as the prohibition of killing another human. Most of us manage compliance with the minimal demand of this principle. The more expansive reading of the catechism is instructive: "To show respect for the life God has given us; to work and pray for peace; to bear no malice, prejudice, or hatred in our hearts; and to be kind to all the creatures of God" (BCP, p. 848).

The "right" to life carries the concomitant responsibility to respect all life given by God. To be consistent in this discipline is to pursue peace and reconciliation whenever and wherever impulses tend toward strife and violence. Furthermore, we are reminded that murder has many dimensions.

Taking the life of another person does not by any means exhaust the many ways we can do murder. Murder is defined as "to kill unlawfully or with malice." Any act that kills the spirit of another human being falls under this principle. Physically, emotionally, or psychologically abusing another human being qualifies as murderous. Maliciously attacking or undermining another person's life and welfare by our slander, gossip, or cruelty does, too. Diminishing or ignoring another may be socially acceptable but is theologically and morally reprehensible. Kindness and respect to all God's creatures is the countervailing responsibility to any "right" to life in any dimension.

Just as murder entails more than homicide, the tenet "You shall not commit adultery" (Exodus 20:14) involves more than sexual infidelity. Even the prayer book paraphrase, to "use all our bodily desires as God intended" (p. 848), is inadequate to encompass this principle.

Our Hebrew ancestors held strong convictions on the matter of purity. The integrity of a thing was not to be compromised by mixing it with another thing. Hence, when Daniel interpreted a dream for Nebuchadnezzar, he likened a kingdom's lack of integrity to the mixing of iron and clay, an extreme hyperbole but effective for indicating how two substances can be severely compromised by mingling (Daniel 2). At a more homely level, for example, different fibers were not to be interwoven (Deuteronomy 22:11). Strict adherence to such principles eventuated in an elaborate system of dietary and cultural disciplines still observed by some communities of Judaism.

Oaths and promises were likewise subject to principles of purity. As might be expected, a people who perceived their relationship to God to be premised upon a promise—a covenant—held all oaths to a high standard.

While Christians depart from most of the social, legal, and dietary particularities derived from this principle, the basic premise is still operative in the formation of a whole (holy) life. Wholeness, the basis of holiness, is still a matter of integrity. This seventh principle, then, extends well beyond the realm and status of marriage.

Any Christian's consideration of this principle begins with the primary promises of the believer's relationship with God: baptism. In the baptismal rite, after confessing belief in the creedal statements received from our tradition (BCP, p. 304), the baptismal candidate promises, with God's help, to remain faithful in the community's life through participation in fellowship, eucharistic worship, and prayer; to resist evil and practice repentance in failure; to proclaim by word and deed the goodness of God in one's own life; to seek and serve Christ in love for all people; and to strive for justice and peace, respecting each person's dignity.

That's an expansive promise. Within each component and throughout the whole there is ample room for compromise, and adultery—the corruption of the promises' integrity—is commonplace. What does it matter that I neglect the community, and who'll notice my absence from worship? Who cares that I twist a truth, and am I really to be blamed for the pain my words inflict? Why shouldn't I take full credit for my accomplishments, and why does it matter that I acknowledge God's role in my well-being? Who has time or energy to go out of the way to care what happens to that person on the street; isn't it obvious that their own choices have led them to this end? One by one, each alibi refutes the baptismal pledge. Multiplied day in and day out, we're all adulterers many times over.

Of course, the implications of this principle extend to marriage, to the pledge to keep oneself, in the intimacy of sexual intercourse, only to one's partner. But the wider applicability touches each person's responsibility, not just those living within the marriage covenant. The responsibility of purity, of integrity, courses through all our relationships, all our lives. We are to be careful, in the most literal sense, of every promise we make, for we are children of promise. Our lives, as believers, depend literally upon the integrity of promise, the wholeness and fullness of God's promise to us.

To embrace this expansive definition of adultery is to enter a realm of unadulterated, transparent honesty. The concluding trinity of principles brings us to this realm and takes us to its center. Therefore, the simple command "You shall not steal" (Exodus 20:15) takes us well beyond larceny. The catechetical expectation is that we "be honest and fair in our dealings; seek justice, freedom, and the necessities of life for all people; and to use our talents and possessions as ones who must answer for them to God" (BCP, p. 848).

It is not enough that I keep my hands to myself, that I avoid taking things that do not belong to me. Being dishonest and unfair in my dealings is theft of trust. More than a matter of personal integrity, honesty and fairness are matters of social, communal integrity. The assumption that my life and actions are disconnected from the wholeness of God's creation is a repudiation of my fundamental belief that God made all things seen and unseen, that all creation is united and related in this common genesis in God.

Therefore, when I buy a product bearing a particular label, even if I render full payment of the item, I may still be guilty of theft. I am not readily aware of the product's provenance, or what it represents. The name on the product may belong to a family no longer in control of the product's manufacture. The product may bear the name of an American family, be produced in Mexico under specifications dictated by a laboratory in France, and owned by a conglomerate in Japan. A controversial anti-drug ad campaign serves as a good example of life's radical connectedness and our complicity in sin. One ad pictures an innocent young person's face with the caption "Last weekend I worked on my car, hung out with a few friends, and helped murder a family in Colombia. C'mon, it was a party." Another similar photo bears the caption "Yesterday afternoon I did my laundry, went for a run, and helped torture someone's dad" (see www.theantidrug.com). The message of the ads is that the purchase and use of illicit drugs support a chain of nefarious, and murderous, actions well beyond the familiar defense "What's the problem? I'm not hurting anybody." While this is an extreme example, we learn with increasing frequency that the seemingly innocent purchase of food and clothing can link us, unwittingly, to sweat shops, child labor, and substandard wages and labor practices in undeveloped countries, and in our own—as investigations into migrant farm labor, poultry processing, and textile production have revealed.

Can we reasonably be expected to achieve perfection in this, or any realm, of human activity? No, for omniscience is beyond our scope. But each of us could be far more mindful of this principle. We make a good beginning in the constant awareness and acknowledgment that we really own nothing. All our talents and possessions are, in truth, gifts abundantly provided by that same God who made us and makes all things. Such an awareness, while it may not keep us from sin, can certainly temper our daily lives and increase in us a lively sense of responsibility, which is the ultimate purpose of all these principles.

This awareness might also lead us to "speak the truth, and not to mislead others by our silence" (BCP, p. 848), as the catechism reframes the ninth principle, "You shall not bear false witness against your neighbor" (Exodus 20:16). Of a piece with the eighth principle, the ninth encourages an integrated honesty, a responsible realism and commitment to what God's people believe to be true—that life in God's community entails a responsibility to honesty about others and honesty with others. Which honesty leads us to the tenth and final principle against covetousness (Exodus 20:17).

Again, while the catechetical interpretation amplifies, it does not fully satisfy. There is more to this principle than to "resist temptations to envy, greed, and jealousy; to rejoice in other people's gifts and graces" (BCP, p. 848). My desire for or jealousy of anything that is given to another is more than possessive greed. It is repudiation of all that I have been given. It implies that God has not met my own sufficiency, that what I have is not enough, that what I am is not enough.

How much is enough? This may be one of the most important questions of our time, especially among those of us privileged to be given so much. To have enough is to have all; sufficiency is security. Whether grasping for more power, lusting for more pleasure, working for more money, or rushing to save more time, we are driven, ultimately, by in innate incompleteness, an abiding sense of not enough.

The ten principles of wisdom bequeathed us by our ancient ancestors begin in an assertion of an abundant God and conclude with an adjuration against grasping insecurity. If we believe in this God, we shall manifest that belief in a life that fully integrates this conviction into the fabric of our living. The proof is in the pudding; the tree is known by the fruit it bears. Whatever cliché one offers, the end is integrity. Belief is not knowing once and for all, not a matter of mere statement; saying does not make it so. Belief is to faith as wedding is to marriage; I commit to belief but live in faith as one commits to wedding but lives in marriage. The proof of love is not in the professing, but in the living.

How, then, shall I love God? In consistency, in integrity, in embracing the fullness of life and love given me by God. By living as one loved by God, as one in and for whom that love is enough.

6

Why Bother?

OUR HEARTS ARE RESTLESS, said Saint Augustine, and shall find no rest until they rest in God. This restlessness is both the source of frustration and the motivation of faith's continuing activity.

The source of that frustration is inherent in the catechetical question, "Since we do not fully obey (the ten commandments), are they useful at all?" Which is another way of asking, "Why bother?" Our restlessness craves a destination, a result and reward. Like the child squirming in expectant agitation, we want to know how long, how much farther, when?

One of the paradoxes of Christian life is the tension between the conviction that God wills all things to goodness, that God is working out God's own magnificent purpose, and the opposing—and maddening—confidence in human progress. The conviction that God wills all things to good is challenged in every tragedy. Why do we suffer disease and natural disaster? Where was God when the child was abused, the loved one struck down? Why do mad, bad things happen to good people? The conviction that every day in every way we are getting better and better—the myth of human progress—is challenged in every revelation that the more things change, the more they stay the same; we only seem to make progress; in truth, our capacity for evil grows side by side with our accomplishment for good.

So, why bother with the commandments?

For the same reason we bother with maps and watches. We could and probably would get by just fine without either; generations before us certainly did. But as our awareness of ourselves and our world grew, so did the need for boundaries, standards, directions, references. In other words, as we grew in relationship, as we and our world expanded, so did our need to mark our place and our path.

The Decalogue (literally, the ten words or sayings) represents essential guidelines, ideals. They are standards, principles. They represent the accumulated experience and wisdom of a particular community that perceived and continues to believe itself in particular relationship with a particular God. As such, and for this particular community, the commandments serve as a standard for self-evaluation and definition. That is, the commandments establish the expectations of relationship in community and define membership within that community.

Like all ideals, standards, and guidelines, the commandments provide a standard for self-evaluation, marking progress and regress, neither of which should become an obsession. It is especially important not to lose sight of the personal nature of these wise standards. Whether that "self" is an individual or a self-identified community like the church, the commandments are presented by a particular God to a particular person, Moses, for a particular people, Israel. The standards are not universal. This particularity is part of the power of the commandments.

The Decalogue represents the fruit of a preexisting relationship. It is a relationship that has sustained several generations of experience, from the episodes of Adam and Eve, Cain and Abel, to Noah to Babel to Pharaoh and Egypt, Moses and Miriam. These are not simply arbitrary rules dropped unilaterally from heaven, despite the story that makes them seem so extraterrestrial in their appearing. Even if they are, as depicted, handed directly from God to Moses, they still represent one side of a dialogue; they are a summation of a conversation between God and Israel that has been taking place since the beginning of creation. To employ a commonplace simile, the tablets are the stone equivalent of a Magic-Marker summary on newsprint—a list of ten essential principles derived from centuries of conference between God and the people.

This point is made clear in Deuteronomy 6, the portion immediately following the story of the Decalogue (Deuteronomy 5), where Moses rehearses the foundation for the commandments: "Hear, O Israel: The Lord is our God, the Lord alone. You shall love the Lord our God with all your heart, and with all your soul, and with all your might." This relationship in all its particularity is the context of the commandments.

The commandments, then, are bounded by particularity and intimacy. They are not a standard by which others outside the relationship are to be judged. They do not apply to any relationship except that of God and God's people. This point is to be borne in mind and heart when our restlessness impels us to an aggressive imposition of these principles beyond the bounds.

"Make him share!" is a familiar cry on the children's playground. It's the demand of the child who has been nurtured in a family or community where sharing is a guiding principle. But the recalcitrant child whose resistance to this principle has prompted the outburst may not have been so nurtured and trained; that child may not hold sharing to be a valued principle. What the teacher or parent must adjudicate in this conflict is not merely the imposition of a rule. At the heart of this conflict is the issue of relationship. The teacher or parent must explain that sharing is a principle of participatory belonging: "If you want to play, you must share." But the choice of belonging, and of adhering to the principle, acknowledges and honors the freedom of the child holding the ball.

Like all analogies, this one has its weaknesses, but helps us to understand that a community is not made simply by the imposition of rules. Rules can and do define a community; in the example given, sharing is a condition of belonging to the play group. But beneath the principle defining the group is the relationship that constitutes the group. For the community of Israel simple imposition of and adherence to the rules, in this case the Decalogue, did not make one a member of the community; that was determined by a wholehearted love for God, the God of Israel's creation and deliverance.

Moreover, Israel—a nomadic people dependent upon the hospitality of others—does not seem to expect from or impose upon its hosts the principles that guide its own life. Other nations have their gods and their own principles. That is what distinguishes the peoples from one another. Even early Christianity reveals a capacious tolerance for such difference.

In his first letter to the church at Corinth, Paul offers a dietary example. He is addressing a community of believers located in a major urban center, surrounded by and no doubt related by choice or blood to others who do not share their faith in Jesus. They will have occasion to dine with others and, as has likely been pointed out to Paul, they will be served food previously offered in religious ritual to other gods. Paul advises his correspondents *not* to make their scruples instruments of judgment or advantage; they are advised to eat whatever is placed before them, only refraining when their *host*, either out of consideration for religious discipline or as a test of the disciples' commitment, is at pains to reveal that their meat course has earlier served as sacrifice to someone else's god (1 Corinthians 10:24ff.).

As his advice indicates, whatever principles of belief and purity guide the disciple of Jesus, those principles are not to be wielded as weapons in warfare. Obsessive adherence to the rules leads to competition and pride, superiority and imperialism—and idolatry. Too much of a good thing, in this case, becomes toxic. Perfectionism in the law—whatever the law—leads the individual to exact an impossible standard of themselves. Eventually it can lead to that delusional superiority that presumes oneself to be above the law. When multiplied by community, such overweening perfectionism quickly manifests itself in a rigid fundamentalism and can lead to excessive violence in its insistence upon its own way.

This insistence, whether in a single person or in the many, is propelled by its opposing force: obsession with the law and moral progress will inevitably lead to either competition and pride on the one hand, or to depression and despair on the other. This sad reality is manifest in the tragic examples of prominent religious and political leaders whose moral fervor and principled rigidity are blown apart and rendered defenseless by unseemly, even depraved, acts of immorality—when they are caught literally with their pants around their ankles or their hand in the cash drawer. It is easy to snicker at such manifest hypocrisy and to deride those who claim depression as a factor in their fall, but it is neither a false nor far-fetched claim.

Depression and despair are the destiny of the moral perfectionist, and fear a constant companion. Obsessive moral compulsion leads to compunction; because perfection lies beyond our capacity, its pursuit is futile. Like it or not, life—and human experience—is like laundry: no matter how much we do, there'll always be more to be done. But just as there are those individuals whose compulsive obsession condemns them to wash their hands continually, or launder and relaunder till all is in shreds, so there are those individuals, and communities, who are so captive to the dream of human perfection that they will stop at nothing, including violent terrorism, to enforce compliance upon others, in a vain attempt to eradicate the imperfect from their sphere.

These are not the ways of love, but of fear and of fear's accomplice, anger. We are not, in the main, stupid. We know, if only instinctively, when the smile is strained or the concern feigned. When we are vulnerable, however, the skillful can delude or deceive us, even as they are themselves deluded and deceived. If and when we feel distrust, we are right to respect that instinct. Like other creatures of the animal kingdom, our instincts are attuned to detect fear in ourselves and in others. The gift of reason that distinguishes us from other animals allows us not merely to act upon these feelings, but to reflect upon them. We have the capability to transcend fear and to establish relationship across its boundaries. But we do so only and always at risk. Thus, returning to the image of the angel bearing the torch and the water, our love of God—and God's love of us—cannot depend upon fear of breaking the rules or failing to keep them all, nor can that love depend upon reward for success at keeping any or all of the rules, even perfectly, were that possible.

The moral crusader's faith is not in God, but in the principles. Jesus was at pains to point out this distinction in his own time. Then, as now, the principles—to use a contemporary idiom—"morphed" from means to end. That is, they changed from a means to expressing love for God in relationship and became instead an end in themselves. The keeping of the principles became the sum and substance of relationship. One's relationship was to the law first, and only secondarily—if then—was God included in the equation. Law thus changed from a guiding spirit to a confining, constraining conduit to God.

Right behavior does not equal right relationship. One can live in strict politeness and rigid propriety with another human being. To all appearances the relationship will fulfill all the rules of respect and dignity. But there will be no life there, no compassion, no love. This point courses through the gospel accounts of Jesus' ministry; the first twelve chapters of Mark's gospel are filled with examples of the arguments this point provoked. In the twelfth chapter, Jesus is asked by a scribe to articulate his first principle: "Which commandment is the first of all?" Which commandment, then, is the fundament, the basis upon which all depends?

Jesus answers from scripture, repeating the summary offered by Moses in Deuteronomy: "Hear, O Israel: The Lord is our God, the Lord alone. You shall love the Lord our God with all your heart, and with all your soul, and with all your might." Going beyond the scribe's request, Jesus offers a second principle, derived from Leviticus (19:18), adding, "The second is this, 'You shall love your neighbor as yourself.'"

In the summary combining Levitical and Deuteronomic principles, Jesus establishes, as Moses had before him, that the law is situated always in relationship. Everything begins in relationship with God, with neighbor, with self—a dynamic and essential trinity whose being, arguably, precedes all others, for it is stated and established in scripture itself centuries before theologians spoke of a holy Trinity. In this trinity of God, neighbor, and self, Jesus restores the fullness of relationship as the first, foundational principle. Therefore, whatever other principles may be derived of human experience, all are expressions of love within relationship. The principles are neither the cause nor the condition of relationship. They are, rather, the ways and means of expressing love within relationship. Relationship, then, is not dependent upon the principles, but the other way around—the principles are always and everywhere dependent upon relationship.

Moreover, in appealing to and appending a second principle, Jesus restores self to equal status in this trinity. In this trinity, as in any loving relationship, mutuality and equality are valued. Despite religion's claims, Israel's (and Jesus') God is remarkably democratic. In creation God creates humankind to enjoy co-creator status. God seeks an equality in relationship that we are at pains to deny, like suitors who insist they are not worthy of another's love. Whatever perceptions of worthiness or unworthiness we hold, they are *our* perceptions. God's perceptions seem always to refute ours. When we presume a superiority, God humbles us. When we presume an inferiority, God encourages us. When we assume the worthiness that God accords us, as we do symbolically in the Eucharist, God meets us, embraces us, and feeds us.

This encouragement is itself the heart of the gospel, for the best news of the good news is the news of our worth in God's eyes and estimations. And it truly comes as news to us, even to the most vain of us. We all know (and perhaps ourselves are or have been) one of those people quite full of self. Vanity and self-importance, and the attitudes of entitlement they engender, are seldom what they seem. The vain and self-important are not secure in themselves; their vanity and self-importance are flimsily erected on the shifting sands of image and mercurial public tastes. The antidote to the bully's insecurity or the aloof beauty's snobbery is not humiliation; one cannot force humility upon another. The antidote to human pride is encouragement.

We need encouragement—what our Hebrew ancestors wisely called a "right heart within us." To encourage is literally "to give heart." Only occasionally do we glimpse that right heart within ourselves or within others. When we do catch sight of it we can be sure that the gospel lives there, that the encouragement of God has found a place in this person, in me.

This is the sad, even tragic, mistake of so much religion, even of so much Christianity—that it lacks or denies this essential encouragement. Yes, it is true that we need reminding of our failing, our weakness—that we need reminding of our need. But we need that reminding, that calling into consciousness, only that this need may be brought into relationship with the God who seeks to grant encouragement. Just as I need to be present, and attentive, to actually engage a conversation with you, so must my deepest needs, fears, anxieties be present and attentive to engage conversation with the God who has always a word of encouragement to offer. When my need is babbling on, when my fear is nattering, when my anxiety is wailing, God interrupts with a much needed, "yes, but . . . ." When my heart says I don't, I can't, I won't, God replies to my heart, "Ah, but you do, you can, you will—because I made you, I know what you are, what you are capable of and I love you, I trust you, I believe in you."

On paper, in quiet reading and private meditation, it seems so simple, so transparent, so obvious, so easy. But it isn't, for a host of reasons the community of faith has given the name Sin.

7

Living in Sin

"WHAT IS SIN?" asks the catechism. Such a small word to bear so much. The dictionary tells me that *sin* is an original creation, a word that comes to us pretty much intact from the oldest forms of the English language. It is defined as "offense against God." But I cannot stop there. I can't imagine God being offended, imperiously pouting or worse, throwing a high holy fit, because of something you or I have done.

When I examine the word *offend* I find that it means, literally, "to strike against." That is immensely helpful, and more so when I learn that an offense is "an act of stumbling, something that outrages the moral or physical senses, the act of attacking, the state of being on the attack (as in the offensive side of a team or army)." Thus I see that to offend God does not necessarily mean to displease God so much as it means to engage in combat and conflict with God. Now we're getting somewhere. Maybe even going someplace we've seldom or never seen on our journey in faith.

We have been told that there is no getting around sin, that we are born in sin and can never escape it. But such understanding of sin makes sin seem like some persistent bacteria or genetic flaw. If we could only find the proper antibiotic, we could wipe out sin. If we could only find the proper marker of sin in our genes, perhaps we could breed a perfect human being. Such concepts of sin only distract and drive us more deeply into obsession with this persistent nemesis.

What if, instead, we return to the matter of relationship? I am in relationship with God and God is in relationship with me. And every relationship knows conflict. It is unavoidable. It is part and parcel of each person's uniqueness, individuality. We cannot help it; occasionally, inevitably, in any relationship we're going to "strike against" the other.

Sometimes that collision is accidental, as unintended as the misstep that sends me physically crashing into the other pedestrian who happens to be sharing the sidewalk with me, when my foot catches abruptly on the uneven pavement and propels me careening into the back or arms of the person in front of me. Or that unintentional hurt I inflict on a friend when I make some unthinking, ignorant, or casual remark only to learn that I've deeply offended. It just can't be helped; as the profane bumper sticker so eloquently if crassly puts it, shit (a Middle English word with Old English and Indo-European roots) happens. In my relationship with God, it happens.

Sometimes the accident is on purpose. I push the other person in line out of my way, maybe not even bothering to mask my aggression with a distracted, preoccupied apology in passing. Or I know that what I'm about to say will wound, is intended to knock the wind out of the other, leave them quite literally speechless. Or drive them away, preferably far away and forever so I don't have to see or deal with them again. This stuff happens, too. In my relationship with God it happens.

I can be outrageous, too. Outrage is excess. Outraging the moral or physical senses is a part of every relationship. We all exceed the moral and physical sensibilities when we push the boundaries. It happens when I make excessive demands on another, or when I exceed the appropriate physical boundaries of relationship.

Sometimes it happens unintentionally. Testing the boundaries is a natural, even good, part of every relationship. If we never risked the boundaries, relationship would never grow. Getting past the hurdles is a difficult aspect of any and every good relationship. It occasionally happens that we take one step forward and hit the wall so forcefully we're propelled two or more steps backward, even landing on our butts. Or we hit the wall so forcefully it shatters, leaving us—both of us in the relationship (or all of us, when the circle of relationship is larger)—standing in fear and awe, the sharp shards of brittle barrier arrayed around us. In all such instances, we learn and grow as individuals and communities. We have grown, and God has grown—as Noah's story, among others, evidences.

Our outrageousness is sometimes quite intentional. We are willful creatures by design, by God's design. Any two willful persons in relationship will seek their own ends with or without regard to the will of the other. God knows (quite literally) the strength of my will. God also knows that I can and will exceed the bounds of our relationship; God can count on it, for that is the way God made me. Had God desired otherwise, you and I would never have been created as we are, endowed with such will.

God made you and me "offensive" by nature. We are created and endowed with the ability to stand against God, for such is the nature of relationship. God gives us this power in freedom. But in freedom there is no control.

Freedom—the realm of free—is defined as "the absence of necessity, coercion, or constraint in choice or action." Think on that. No necessity, no coercion, no constraint in choice or action. This is where we live. This is that state we value above all others. In this freedom there is no necessity, coercion, or constraint to "obey the law." Hence, the Decalogue cannot, in freedom, hold us. No law can. Not in freedom. That's the good news.

That's also the bad news. In freedom, power is also free. As in a wrestling match, power can shift from one opponent to another, so in life whatever mastery we have over sin can as quickly turn, giving sin the advantage over us. Those accidental incidences of sin are only a hint of how quickly and unexpectedly the tables can be turned.

"How does sin have power over us?" asks the catechism. If sin is offense against God—pitting my will against God's will, striking my will, my self, against God—then sin's ultimate power over us is manifest most fully in the conviction that this contentious opposition is itself the ultimate good. To put it another way, sin's ultimate power is evidenced in my presumption of the rightness of my own will, the superiority of my will, my desire, my design. Sound familiar? It should. Remember Adam?

Adam's, Eve's, and our sin is one and the same. We don't want a mutual relationship of equality with God; we want to be God. We want it all and we want to be boss of it all. Relationship demands a sharing of wills, a give and take, an interdependence. That takes work. So does pursuing our own will, so much work it qualifies as slavery.

The Christian image of the power of sin is slavery, an image actually holding very little meaning for most of us privileged (and I do mean privileged) to live when, where, and as we do in much of the developed world. But slavery is still the right word, for it means simply "submitting to a dominating influence." Who me?

A simple and common example will suffice. I love my work, and there's plenty of it. I take tremendous joy in most of the daily tasks and derive much satisfaction from the extraordinary things I'm invited and asked to do. Much of the time I even feel that I have, if not total control, at least a graspable and secure handle on my work. In other words, most of the time I believe that I have the freedom to control my work.

In this regard I am fortunate. Most of the time. But my love for what I do can easily and often blind me to another reality. If not careful and vigilant, my work can seduce me into more and more activity, deeper and deeper involvement. Soon, I am rushing from one meeting to another, frantically racing to get this task or that one done, pushing to meet that deadline, this appointment. Soon, in the twinkling of an eye, I am no longer the one in control. My work has slipped up on my blind side, seized me securely, and holds me close. I am "submitting to a dominating influence."

Poet and commentator Andrei Codrescu, in an essay of the same title, maintains that "The Devil Never Sleeps." The Devil's too busy to sleep, too busy dealing with his own creation to rest. Whether one believes in an incarnate personification of the demonic or not, Codrescu's Devil is all too apparent and familiar in me and my friends, caught up in the web woven of the ephemeral strands of digital technology, of cellular and cable communications—at the center of which I sit in all my self-importance.

Now substitute will for work. I take tremendous joy in most of the daily challenges put to me and derive much satisfaction from the extraordinary results that come of my creative initiatives and wise counsels. Much of the time I even feel that I have, if not total control, at least a graspable and secure handle on my will. In other words, most of the time I believe that I have the freedom to control my will and use it constructively for good.

In this regard I am fortunate. Most of the time. But my satisfaction easily and often blinds me to another reality. If not careful and vigilant, my will can seduce me into more and more assurance of my rightness and the scope of my authority. Soon, I am taking responsibility for more and more, insisting upon my way as the best or only way, resenting criticism, resisting collaboration, withdrawing into the heights of my own superiority. Soon, in the twinkling of an eye, I am no longer the one in control. My will has slipped up on my blind side, seized me securely, and holds me close. I am "submitting to a dominating influence." I am enslaved to sin, as scripture so eloquently says it.

In her book *Search for Silence*, Elizabeth O'Connor relates the story of a scholarly researcher whose team worked late on an important project. The senior scientist invited his two colleagues home for coffee where, as they relaxed, their conversation ranged widely. The topic turned to Greek architecture, and the host took from the shelf a new volume on the subject.

> [He] and handed it to his more advantaged coworker, who quickly glanced at the pages and returned it to him. He was already putting the book back on the shelf when he glimpsed from the corner of his eye the hand of the other man extended to receive the book. The picture hardly registered. He did not come to terms with what had happened until he was in bed, and then he saw again the hand of the other man reaching to receive the book he had never offered. All unconsciously he had made the judgment that this man, being self-tutored, would not be interested in art. In an automatic way he had excluded him.
>
> The scientist had not thought himself capable of treating another fellow human like this, but he had enough understanding to know that this was not an isolated incident in his life. It was a glimpse of something in himself of which he was only dimly aware. . . . Martin Buber defines sin as our failure to grant to another his plea for community. This was certainly the sin that was dealt with that long night. (O'Connor, *Search for Silence*, [Waco, TX: Word Publishers, 1972], pp. 40–41)

In this slavery more is at stake than the obvious loss of liberty. Substantial as that loss is, it is only a small measure of the damage. As O'Connor's story evidences, the greater loss is relationship, community—the whole trinity of relationships.

Whether under the influence of work, money, power, authority, or any of the myriad ways sin is manifested in our lives, the resulting slavery damages all our relationships. Under submission to any influence, being acted upon instead of freely acting, I become an object, a thing, something less than a person. Even in small doses, slavery is corrosive. It eats at the whole sense of oneself as a full person. Without this integrity, we are disadvantaged in relationships to others, to our neighbor.

Deprived of a full sense of myself, what do I have to offer to my neighbor, to any other person? Whatever relationships I engage in this diminished state are most likely motivated by an abiding sense of need. This need may manifest itself in the arrogant, bullying posture, or the cloying dependency, of the insecure. But at either extreme, or any point between, the possibility and potential of fully mutual relationship is compromised, or denied. It's not that relationship is impossible, but that relationship is impeded. Under submission we still have relationships, but they are distorted. They are relationships that do not honor our or anyone else's integrity.

Slavery in whatever form is not healthy for anyone involved in it. The slave's wholeness is damaged and demeaned, but so is the slaveholder's. So pervasive is the influence of slavery that we know, sadly from our own history, that it is unhealthy for the whole society—our nation's wholeness has been damaged and demeaned so forcefully that over one hundred years after its official abolition, we are still not healed.

Ultimately, according to the summary of the law as Jesus framed it, if we are incapable of estimable self-integrity and denied fully mutual relationship with our neighbor, we cannot possibly know the fullness of relationship with God. Corrosion at the core of the self weakens the entire structure.

How are we loosed from this bondage, released from this slavery, delivered from this submission? The biblical and catechetical term for our restoration to freedom is *redemption*. It's a perfectly good and adequate word, but redemption is an economic term and anything having to do with money is freighted in our understanding. Redemption means, literally, "to buy back," as in paying a ransom. As it stands, the word implies a trade.

I find the word more helpful, and more instructive of God's relationship with me, when divided into its parts. The root of *redemption* is the word *deem*, an Old English word meaning "to judge" or better, "hold or believe." Thus to be re-deemed means to be judged again, to be held and believed again. To be restored to value. Understood in this manner, redemption from sin is not a trade. It is a gift.

This understanding is consistent with a gospel, and a God, of encouragement. I am redeemed from sin in God's continual and continuous, unwavering confidence in me, God's love for me, God's hope in me. I am redeemed by God's belief in me. Because that love is constant, has never changed, is as eternal as Godself, it cannot be bought, traded or otherwise negotiated. Even when enslaved by sin, I am deemed of value in God's eyes and estimation. Though I lose sight of this confidence, though I hide from it or have it hidden from me, it remains.

It remains like the sun, visible at night in the reflected radiance of moon and planets. Even when the sun and moon are hidden by clouds, they are still there, awaiting the passage of time to shine once more. Even if only glimpsed occasionally, briefly, fleetingly, God's confidence in me remains to encourage. No matter how I judge myself, no matter others' estimation of me, God's belief in me remains to re-deem me. God's estimation stands to refute, dispute my own estimation.

We know the power of this re-deeming in our human relationships. We know it in the simplest, most basic of relationships; anyone who has ever known the love of a pet knows this unqualified, unwavering esteem and affection. We know the power of a child's confidence to call forth our best efforts and better instincts. We know the power of a friend's or partner's trust and faith in us to restore us to a balanced sense of our worth in times when we are beaten down (or puffed up). Why should it not be equally, even surpassingly, so of our relationship with God?

Redemption, in this sense, is now and ever has been continuous with the creation itself. God hasn't changed God's mind, or heart, about us or the rest of the creation. Deemed good from its inception, God has always deemed us of worth—worthy of love and confidence. Had we ceased that status in God's estimation, God could and would have been done with us long ago. Yet we have no evidence of any change. God has been and continues to be persistent in love, deeming us valuable and lovable even, and especially, when we were least capable of loving either ourselves or one another.

When early Christians spoke and wrote of the "foolishness" of the cross, the seeming craziness of God (as we believe God to be), this is what they had in mind. This belief we hold—this notion that God can and does love us so inalterably, so consistently, so prodigally— is sheer madness to a world whose economy insists on value for value. But even from the earliest days of our faith's experience of God, it has been maintained that God's ways are not like our ways. God has never given us away, never sold us out; God does not "buy us back." We are not now nor have we ever been for sale. And as for ransom, well, from the standpoint of our economy, at our best we're worth only a few dollars in mineral rights and at our worst we're not worth the powder it would take to blow us away. God's economy, thankfully, is not like our economy.

8

Only Human

MUCH OF THE CONFUSION and conflict at the heart of
Christianity centers in the meaning of one word: Messiah. Disagreement over the definition of this word and
the identity of the person who fulfills this word separates Jews and
Muslims from Christians, and divides Christians themselves. Thus
it must be said at the outset that what I offer on this subject is only one
very personal perspective. It is neither intended nor understood to
be exhaustive.

That being said, however, the personal and particular nature of
this perspective is essential to the Christian understanding of Messiah.
Central to Christian faith is the conviction that ultimately each individual Christian is called to relationship with God. The call of the
people of Israel is acknowledged and celebrated as a significant development in the human understanding of God and of human relationship with God. That God is conceived to have called and entered
into relationship with a particular people represents a radical departure from other theologies of the time. All Jews had access to the relationship through membership in the community, and each Jew was

guaranteed relationship through birth to a Jewish mother. Matrilineal descent was, of course, verifiable in ways that paternity was not. In the case of male Jews, affirmation of identity in the community of believers was sealed in the irreversible removal of the foreskin. Thus the token of commitment was an indelible and undeniable one, but was also intensely personal and private, being made to a part of the body normally hidden from view.

Christianity began as a movement within Judaism. Its adherents honored many of the traditions and much of the theology of Judaism, but there were differences of opinion and departures from accepted norm that grew over time. Much of the first tumultuous century of Christianity was consumed with the nature and particulars of membership in community. Christians, like Jews, affirm a particular call to relationship with God. Christians, however, maintain that *each person* is called by God and that *every person* has access to relationship with God, regardless of that person's community of birth. In the first communities of Christian belief, where adherents were themselves Jewish, this insistence upon access to and affirmation of personal, particular relationship represented a development as significant and controversial as the earlier theology of particularity that had distinguished Jews from other religionists of their time. But these differences were fairly negotiable until believers outside the Jewish community—Gentiles (a common name for any and all non-Jews)—claimed access to and affirmation of the same belief in personal relationship with God. Details of the debate and the first council of church leadership convened to deal with it are found in the Book of the Acts of the Apostles.

In that narrative we learn that some communities of early Christian believers accepted Gentiles into membership, provided those males submitted to circumcision in token of their commitment. Strict adherence to this and other Jewish laws was for some Christian communities a requisite to membership. As the teaching of Christianity spread and Gentile interest and participation increased, the question of such practices arose and became a matter of contention. Those who insisted upon strict adherence to Jewish fundamentals stood at one extreme and those who advocated a more liberal, metaphorical position argued that baptism sufficed to signify full membership. Leaders of the scattered churches gathered in Jerusalem to debate and deliberate the issue. Paul, Barnabas, Peter, and others offered their experiences and perspectives, drawn from their missions. James, leader of the church in Jerusalem, was appointed judge and arbiter. His ruling, which became normative, advocated expansiveness and liberality, opening the community of Christian belief to any person who committed to personal relationship with God and sealed that commitment in baptism.

This ruling did not settle the matter. This is obvious from the continuing references to the issue in letters included in the Christian scriptures. The experience of civil rights in American society and the ordination of women in the Episcopal Church serve as comparable examples. In both issues, a rigidly strict exclusionary position was legislatively overruled by a liberally inclusive one. A new norm was advocated, allowed, and in many places enacted. But the struggle continues long after the decision is rendered.

This is the nature of relationship. Difference — otherness — is essential to relationship. Conflict and struggle are inevitable. This difference, like the tension between birth and death that gives each human life its vitality, is the dynamic that gives every relationship its life. Possessing power to invigorate and power to destroy, the outcome of the dynamic struggle is, in every relationship, a mixture of the two. Sustaining balance in any relationship is not a unilateral enterprise or achievement. Whether moving rhythmically with a partner on the dance floor or negotiating the demands of daily life with God, the bottom line is the same — each of us in the relationship must be mindful of and sensitive to each other, and to everyone and everything else around us, if we are to remain upright, much less in sync.

Because Christianity maintains that each person is called by God and that every person has access to relationship with God, regardless of that person's community of birth, then Christianity must, and usually does, acknowledge and celebrate the distinctive nature of this personal relationship. Christianity affirms that one's relationship with and accountability to God are ultimately particular. That is to say, in the end, one's relationship with God will not be determined by or based upon membership in any particular community, nor will it be determined by or based upon adherence to or completion of any set of practices.

At one level, then, Christianity is intensely personal, private, and potentially isolating. This is the challenge of Christian faith—that it is so personal, that it demands so much responsibility of the individual. This is also the merit of Christianity—that it acknowledges the burden of human life and experience. Neither being human nor being Christian is easy. Each demands much of us, not least that we accept full responsibility for our lives. We undertake this challenge "with fear and trembling" (Philippians 2:12).

This responsibility does not come all at once, nor are we helpless. Ideally, from infancy we are surrounded by parents, family, community, teachers, mentors, and a host of other resources to nurture and guide us. They carry the weight of responsibility for us and with us, only gradually entrusting it to us as we mature. Thus we are taught how to be responsible, how to bear what is demanded of us. We are also taught the demands of relationship, learning how to be sons and daughters, brothers and sisters, companions and colleagues, and in time, how to be parents and all the other relational roles available to us.

But how are we to be all that relationship with God demands of us? Christians believe that God does not leave us dangling, does not leave us orphaned (John 14:18). Christians believe that God nurtures us in relationship in and through the person of Jesus. Thus the Christian who affirms relationship with God personally affirms Jesus as Messiah and commits to a particular, personal relationship with Jesus. The nature of particular relationship is an inscrutable uniqueness; the bond that unites two persons in relationship is a mystery even for the two.

The most powerful scriptural image of Jesus for me is that of brother (Hebrews 2:11). Truly, it is all I need to establish the fullness and the mystery of Jesus. Perhaps because I have two brothers and two sisters this image speaks to me in ways denied the only or orphaned child. Being the eldest of the five children in my family, I am particularly attuned to Jesus' role as my elder brother. The elder brother is the one who experiences life a few steps ahead of the younger sibling. Each may share the same or similar experience, but one has gone before. More importantly, spoken or not, there is assurance in the power of survival; the older sibling has been through the experience and lived.

I accept Jesus as Messiah.

That statement does not exhaust my affirmation of faith, but it is central to it. The catechism asks, "What is meant by the Messiah?" For the moment, let's remove the definite article, *the*, and consider the meaning of the word *Messiah*.

A very complex word, messiah can be approached through a progression of synonyms. Very simply, messiah means "anointed." Anointing is the practice of ritually smearing oil on a person to signify that person's being set apart for a particular purpose. This practice, known as "consecration" (literally, to make sacred) was the ancient rite by which kings and priests were acknowledged and ordained for service.

Sacred is a synonym for *holy*. *Holy* is a synonym for *whole*, which is a synonym for *entire*. This progression is central to my own understanding of messiah as one who is acknowledged and called to wholeness.

Wholeness is a component of every Christian vocation; each of us is called into a relationship with God as whole human beings. God does not expect or require that we be other than what we are created to be, wholly human. But who shall mentor me in wholeness? By what standard do I mark my maturity into human wholeness?

I accept, acknowledge, and understand Jesus to be the one human being uniquely created, particularly called, and specifically ordained to fulfill this vocation and ministry. This was and is Jesus' vocation, his life's work. I acknowledge Jesus as the perfect human, not because I believe he never made a mistake. I suspect he made as many mistakes as you or I make in a lifetime; to err is, after all, human. Indeed, Jesus would not be a "whole" human being otherwise. His vocation was of greater significance than to model right behavior or good manners.

Perhaps it's the democrat in me, but I readily embrace Jesus as *primus inter pares*, as "first among equals." As my elder brother, he is in every way like me, but occupies a primacy if only because of the precedence of his birth. If there be an eternal dimension to his vocation, it is that Jesus is everything God desired and dreamed humans might be. Born in time centuries later than Adam, Jesus is older than Adam himself in that Jesus lives the life Adam failed to fulfill. Jesus is the embodiment of God's creative desire for humans.

As such, Jesus bears full responsibility for all that it means to be human. He is born without entitlement, is nurtured in exile. He struggles as we do. Whether in mythic contest with a satanic tempter in the desert on the eve of his ministry or sweating in combat with his own will in a garden on the eve of his death, he lives a life so fully like my own that I am bound to him by compassion, literally the suffering he shares with me, the human life he bears with me.

Of the mysteries surrounding him, Jesus' divinity is the most fathomable. If all the world, if everything seen and unseen is created by God, what can be more divine than that which lives fully into God's design and intention? Any such creature needs no greater connection to God, no greater claim. In fully realizing, in wholly fulfilling all that God intends for the human creature, Jesus is divine. Moreover, Jesus calls us into that same divinity, urges us draw closer to the same God he himself called father and acknowledged as lord.

Jesus encourages us to draw near to God, to trust the God he knew and proclaimed as "Abba," the affectionate, intimate term whose nearest equivalent in our own language is "Daddy." What a leap, what audacity to move from the majesty of the Creator drawn in Genesis to a God so approachable, so familiar. This invitation to relationship with God is called *atonement,* a simple word, a synonym for *reconciliation.*

Various doctrines of Christian atonement have been ventured by successive generations of believers. These differing opinions of how and why the life and death of Jesus affect reconciliation between God and humankind separate communities of believers, and individual believers within particular Christian communities, from one another. Probably the only point of agreement among them all is that each and every attempt to explain or understand the particulars of this relationship brings us always to mystery. Why should we expect a difference between this relationship and any other we know in human experience? Is it not true of every relationship that, at its heart, we come to mystery?

It is this dynamic not-knowing that draws us into relationship. It is this dynamic not-knowing that keeps and sustains us in relationship. This is the drama of relationship, the engagement in another's life and the engagement with another's life that bring divergent lives into communion, a rich give and take that piques interest and curiosity and weaves the strands of interest into a common thread, yet seems never to come to final fulfillment, but continually opens to a new vista and invites us into a new journey.

Getting to and growing in relationship is a gradual process of maturation. We are, of course, always in relationship. The elemental biological prerequisites to human life relate us from before birth to the mother whose egg and the father whose sperm carry the genetic material from which we are formed. The mysterious meeting of one egg of many with one sperm cell of millions in a particular moment is our own experience of *kairos,* the Greek name for the other dimension of time, separate from but within *chronos.* Chronological time is measured on watches and calendars, by the rising and setting of sun and moon, the rotation of earth and movement of tides. Kairos is the mysterious, and for believers, the holy convergence of elements and events. Kairos is always fulfillment, the gathering of seemingly disparate components of life into a whole, hence the "holiness" of kairos. In such moments, the believer perceives the palpable, even practical, presence of mystery. In such moments the believer perceives the active presence of God, the expressive handiwork of the creative mystery still engaged with human enterprise and experience. For the believer in Israel's God there is no such thing as fate, only the abiding relationship with a God who, like our earthly partners, is sometimes very near, sometimes seen and known, sometimes very far, sometimes unseen and unknown but always present with us in the rich history we share, in the mystery of future we daily approach.

Therefore, from conception in the womb and, for the believer, in the mystery that precedes even that entry into time's reality, we are always in relationship. Each of us is, like our God, bound in a trinity of relationship — relationship with God, with neighbor, and with self. The vicissitudes of all relationship situate us in a maelstrom of change. We're never truly at peace, in stasis. My sense of myself is a complex and simultaneous mixture of satisfaction, disappointment, accomplishment, disgust, rest, agitation, order, anxiety, and security. My relationship with my neighbor, which is to say, everyone other than me, is as complex and demanding. So is my relationship with God, who can be and is everything I imagine and far more.

So while I do not agree with every notion of the atonement with God accomplished by and in Jesus, I concede that all the orthodox doctrines and probably most of the heretical ones, too, are likely at least partly true — if one is prepared to accept any human perception as valid to the perceiver. To use a human analogy, in my childhood I sometimes perceived my parents' decisions and disciplines to be mean and cruel; that was how I perceived them. And while I have grown in adulthood to appreciate that their decisions and disciplines often led to my own betterment and welfare, I know also that my parents are human and that on some occasions they could be and probably were cruel, if not in those particular incidents I recall, but in some measure, somewhere.

I find some theological doctrines of atonement unacceptably cruel and ugly. To believe that God might create a child, any child, for the express and exclusive purpose of sacrifice is intolerable to me. Yet, I can understand how God might be perceived in such a light. And I can accept, and even believe, that God could be so cruel. Evidently, I am not alone in this capacity; only a brief sojourn in the Hebrew scriptures reveals that God's bloodthirsty cruelty was perceived by our ancestors to be an attribute of the divine. Fear of God, awe before God, respect of God are based not simply upon God's majesty and scope of beneficent accomplishment. God has been and still is feared, awesome (and awful), and respected out of our legitimate fear for our own safety in this God's presence.

I know what it is to fear a father, for my own father was a strict disciplinarian with a volatile temper. My father's and my mother's parents and cultures routinely employed child-rearing practices that, by contemporary standards, would be considered extreme. Their use of corporal punishment would probably be deemed cruel and even, by some, abusive. I have recalled quite vividly on preceding pages, an instance in which I provoked my father to strike me. It was one of those moments when our violent tempers clashed, when I said something that triggered a reflex to slap. I was by no means a child; I was an insolent teenager, and in retrospect, I know I deserved the blow that inflicted more humiliation than pain, and no lasting damage beyond the red mark that was gone by supper time.

After the air and our emotions had cooled, my father came to me and apologized with a remorse I knew to be genuine by the rare tears that accompanied it. Even now as I see his face in memory, I believe I know what God's face looked like as he placed the rainbow over Noah. Indeed, I rather suspect the rainbow was itself an afterthought, a visible reminder of the sun's refraction through God's own tears made to remind God ever thereafter of the remorse God's own anger occasioned.

Today, as I reflect upon the life, death, and resurrection, I believe them to be inseparable components of what I believe of atonement. They cannot be considered apart from one another. Jesus' life as the human created and called to embody, to incarnate, the will of God for all humanity would, in any case, have included death, for that is essential to a whole human life. The manner of that death, however, was his and ours to determine within the freedom God allows.

Those who espouse sacrificial and/or substitutionary doctrines of atonement find the story of Abraham and Isaac (Genesis 22) supportive of these perspectives. This narrative portrays God's testing Abraham by demanding that Abraham take his only son, Isaac, to a remote place. There, Abraham is commanded to build an altar, to bind the boy, lay him upon the prepared altar, and slaughter and burn the boy's body as in any animal sacrifice. In obedience to God, Abraham does as commanded, is ready to demonstrate his faith. His arm raised above his head ready to take Isaac's life, Abraham is stayed by the voice of an angel who issues the reprieve and directs Abraham's attention to a ram caught in a nearby thicket, a substitute for the beloved Isaac.

This story seems to presage the experience of Jesus, to a degree. But there are significant differences. Isaac was innocent, and ignorant, of his fate; Jesus was quite aware and thoughtful about what was demanded of him. Isaac was passive and bound; he went unwillingly to the altar. Jesus was active and free, willingly embracing the vocation to which God called him. In fact, if the story of Abraham and Isaac were treated purely analogically, and allegorically, then the outcome is a bit different from what Christians have traditionally maintained.

When compared to the story of Jesus, in the Genesis tale Abraham represents God; Isaac represents the descendants of Adam, the people of God—for the people surrounding Jesus are all ignorant of the drama in which they are caught up. The gospel of Mark actually posits that God intentionally hid the true mission and identity of Jesus from them, willing their ignorance. In the gospels it's the people themselves who are bound by sin and placed on the altar of sacrifice, with God's unseen arm raised to plunge the knife. Jesus is the one substituted at the last minute, the sacrificial lamb snared in life's thorny thicket.

The story of Jonah suggests a different possible outcome. Jonah is dispatched by God to bring the people of Nineveh to full relationship with God. Jonah resists that call, flees from it. But eventually God prevails and Jonah goes to Nineveh where, to his surprise and consternation, the people embrace God. In that story and its surprise ending we see that humans do not always behave as predicted. Ironically, in this story no one behaves as expected. Jonah the prophet behaves badly. The sailors who are nearly killed by Jonah's rebellion against God and the storm it provokes actually show a deep religious conviction and a concern for Jonah's welfare, until they are convinced to remand Jonah to God's care by tossing him overboard.

Jonah, who seems determined to be a martyr to his own convictions, is instead delivered safe and sound to his mission. The Ninevites whom Jonah has dismissed as heathen instead prove faithful, frustrating Jonah's sweeping stereotypical judgment of Israel's enemies as unworthy of God's attention or love. And finally, the prophet who should have rejoiced in Nineveh's embrace of God retires to a lonely place and stews in bitterness, angry that God's confidence in Nineveh has proven justified and his own estimations of Nineveh's potential for repentance and redemption have proven wrong.

Jesus' call to bring all people to God is more similar to Jonah's call, if on a grander scale, than it is to Isaac's fate. Jesus, however, unlike Jonah, embraced his vocation and took it up willingly. As Jesus preached and worked among the people, it was his hope that those who encountered him would find and be brought to full relationship with God. Thus he pursued his mission until its waning days, when it became clear that what he sought would not be fulfilled by his work alone. This heartbreaking realization pervades the final days of his life.

In the gospels of Matthew, Mark, and Luke the Transfiguration seems to mark the point of a change in awareness and orientation. In each of those gospels, as Jesus stands upon the mount, the road leads literally downhill to Jerusalem, a city of danger for him. In all the gospels, Jesus' entry into Jerusalem—and the exuberantly militant welcome of him so at odds with his own preaching and teaching—

made clear to him the failure of his mission. In a sad asymmetry to the Ninevites, the deeper into our life Jesus enters, the more determined we become to deny his mission and ministry. The closer God draws to us in Jesus, the more violent our repellence. Right up to the last night of his life, Jesus contends with the clash between his will and what he perceives so clearly to be God's will; shall Jesus, like Jonah, persist in his own way, or shall he literally go with the flow, submitting to the natural consequences of humanity's obstinate resistance of its own freedom over against God?

Every Christian knows how badly this chapter ends, how violently Jesus dies—as a consequence not just of our non-acceptance of God, but of our determined desire to be completely free of God, to end the relationship once and for all. So we succeed in killing the relationship. Jesus dies, his death the clash and consequence of God's will and ours. Jesus dies because we and our human institutions have willed it, and because God wills that we shall have such freedom. God will not intervene. No angel cries out; no ram magically appears to take his place. Jesus dies, son of man, son of God. The relationship is destroyed, the covenant shattered. The veil of the Temple is torn asunder; the earth itself trembles. God's heart is broken.

But this is only part of the story. Crucifixion is followed by resurrection. Those who come to the tomb find that the man declared dead and sealed securely in earth's embrace is loose and living. The story returns us all to the tale's ancient beginning; Adam is fashioned of earth and Jesus is entombed in and raised from the earth, in gardens. God who made Adam of the earth has raised, restored Jesus to life from the earth. Jesus' vocation to humanity, like Job's, has been tried and vindicated. Jesus' confidence, Jesus' faith in God, like Jesus himself, has survived even death.

The story comes full circle, however, only in the unfolding of days thereafter. In reassuring companionship Jesus urges those who encounter him to go beyond their fear, encourages them to see what God has revealed, is revealing, in and through him. He is with them for forty days, leading them on the exodus through the wilderness of grief and suspicion, sadness and skepticism, until he disappears from them for good. Then, on the fiftieth day after his resurrection, the believers are seized by a new spirit, an awakened awareness.

As they gather, they begin to tell of God's mighty deeds in their own lives (Acts 2). Gradually and yet suddenly they are aware that they are speaking of the same God, they are sharing relationship with the same God. They are, each one and all at the same time, in union with their God. And they are whelmed.

Whelmed. That's the old English word for "turned over, flipped." They are not overwhelmed, submerged, but just the opposite. They are flipped over and reoriented, the way one feels when a long-held perception has been suddenly flipped on its head, proven wrong. They are at one with God, in full and joyful relationship. The worst that could happen has come to pass, and gone. They and all like them who participated in Jesus' rejection and death, they who deserved themselves to die, were free, alive, filled with joy.

9

Only Child

A FTER PENTECOST, those believers who had found common bond in their experience of Jesus were faced with a considerable challenge: Just *who* was this Jesus? While they could find similarity, even unity, in their experiences of this person, they had yet to situate this person in their shared contexts of time and space.

Much like us, they resorted to the language of kinship; Jesus was someone's son, was a person born into a familial lineage. The gospels of Matthew and Luke offer concrete, if contradictory, genealogies. The Matthean history (1:1–17) traces Jesus' patrimony back through David to Abraham, while the Lucan account (3:23–38) follows the trajectory all the way back to "Adam, son of God." Despite centuries of doctrine that construe the role of Joseph as surrogate, both of these gospel genealogies clearly claim Joseph as the sire of Jesus. Both accounts entitle Jesus to claim the name "Son of Man." Nor does Jesus ever repudiate his relationship to Joseph.

Still, those who met and knew Jesus strained to give expression to what they had experienced in him, how and why he was distinctive. To say that Jesus was "Son of God" was, as is seen in Luke's history, no more distinctive than the name "Son of Man." Every descendant of Adam is entitled to claim descent from God's self-giving creation of life and a place within the family of humanity.

As they struggled to give utterance to the ineffable, our ancestors in faith appended a distinctive qualifier to describe Jesus; for them he was the *only* Son of God. What does it mean to say that Jesus is the *only* Son of God? The assertion is certainly *not* one of biology; even the gospel accounts seem content to affirm the full humanity of Jesus, an essential affirmation that has sometimes been obscured by the insubstantial claims of a vaporous divinization that removes Jesus from the daily, dirty business of humanness.

This brings us to the matter of gender: Jesus was male. To ask why is to beg the question; beyond the accidental mysteries of human conception why should we import any more meaning to this reality than we do in our own lives? All our ancestors knew, all that we know, and all that is needed is that the historical person at the center of our inquiry and relationship was/is a gendered male named Jesus.

In a fascinating book misleadingly titled *The Sexuality of Christ in Renaissance Art and in Modern Oblivion* (University of Chicago Press, 1996), art historian Leo Steinberg reveals how the many paintings of the nude infant Jesus center on the child's genitalia—the incontrovertible and incarnational evidence of his *humanness*. Nor was this emphasis artistic license; Steinberg finds compelling evidence that the same theme dominated theology, doctrine, and preaching in the Vatican, which during the Renaissance was the institutional center of the community of the church. This intentional attention suggests a needful corrective. Whenever our proclivities incline us to make Jesus someone or something different from ourselves—to make him the exception, and thus exempt ourselves from full participation in his life—we are brought back to the central affirmation of his ordinariness, his humanness.

This ordinary humanness is central to the "only-ness" of Jesus. What distinguishes Jesus as the *only* Son of God is his fulfillment of all that it means to be human. In this regard, Jesus does not simply inherit the title of Adam as "Son of God," Jesus supplants Adam—becomes the "new Adam"—in whose life God's intentions are realized. Thus to say that Jesus is the "only" son of God is not to claim that Jesus is the *sole* son of God. Rather, it is to claim that *only* Jesus reveals the fullness of God's creative intention for human being. In so doing, Jesus earns also the name "Divine."

It is a mistake to think that a divine thing or creature is somehow other-worldly. Divinity does not remove anyone or anything from the temporal realm. Today we would deem it archaic, or even "camp," to say of someone or something, that they or it is *divine*. Yet I would argue our need to recover this perfectly accurate usage of the word *divine*. For once upon a time, the word divine denoted a perfection rooted in the Bible, a perfection of embodied wholeness. To say, as one once could (without risk of embarrassment) that a particular rose was "divine," was to say this flower embodies, real-izes, the wholeness of "rose-ness"—it is the incarnation of what we mean by the word *rose*.

Anyone, or anything, who thus embodies—incarnates—the fullness of being is, indeed, divine. That person or thing that truly real-izes—makes real—the fullness of God's creation is divine. This is the goal of vocation, to live fully into all that God has made us to be. And we have been made human. Neither more nor less. Nor is anything more, or less, expected or demanded of us. Those who met Jesus claimed they had encountered a human of rare, exceptional, integrity. He was not simply a moral person, a good person. He was human integrity itself, all that we perceive a whole person to be, the fullest—only—incarnate realization of God's intention in the making of humankind.

Those who encountered Jesus and knew him, those who encounter and know him still, proclaim that Jesus is the only perfect image of the Creator God, that he shows us the nature of God. Why should we deem such an assertion exceptional? Each of us embodies and is shaped by our deepest relationships. We suspect, for example, that deeply troubled pathologies are the result of faulty parenting and abusive relationships. Should it be any wonder that those who experience profoundly loving parents and just relationships might reflect something of those who have so shaped them?

When I look in the mirror I see my mother's face; when I clear my throat, I hear my father's familiar habit. When I prepare a meal, I see my mother's hands at work; when I weigh a dilemma and find a just and balanced way, I perceive my father's judgment. I am fortunate to have become my mother, my father—fortunate to have so known such love and wisdom, and occasionally blessed to impart it to others through my own life. Their very natures are visible in me, and though you may never meet them, to know me is in significant measure to know them.

The nature of God is revealed in Jesus, not because God somehow contravened the orders of creation in some extraordinary way, but because Jesus felt keenly and lived fully into the relationship all humans, every human, is invited to share with the God who is love. Ironically, even sadly, some of the catechetical language pertaining to our human inheritance has proven the most distancing.

The trouble with God, the trouble with Jesus, the trouble with any relationship is our tendency to confuse particularity with exclusivity. Sorting the claims of the particularity of one's relationships from the genuinely sinful tendencies to selfishness and jealousy demands perpetual, painstaking discipline.

Whether our relationship be with God, with Jesus, with a beloved spouse or partner, with a parent, sibling, or child, we tend toward the selfish desire to have that person all to ourselves, and to jealousy of any sharing of that person with others. In the matter of our relationship to God and/or Jesus, those proclivities can (and do) lead us into claims or assertions that are less about the other than they are about our inability and unwillingness to share, our woeful insecurity and our lack of trust in the limitless capacities of God's love.

What does it mean to say that Jesus was conceived by the power of God and became incarnate from Mary? No more or less than can be said of any human being, whose conception and birth are a combination of mechanics and mystery. But why this particular human conception and birth?

The question only makes sense in a much longer story of a loving, creator God—as the ultimate expression of progressive revelation, the gradual unfolding of love in a relationship enduring millennia. Like the progressive revelation of human love, which is a combination of word and deed, the relationship of God and humankind employs many expressions. The infant perceives love as self-centered welfare—clean diapers, the comfort of clothes and bedding, food and drink. Gradually words supplement action, and "I love you" enters the vocabulary as a phrase subject to many meanings, some clarified and others confused by experience. The ultimate expressions of love, however, are manifest in self-giving, the ultimate love being wholly disinterested or, as Jesus presented in parable and person, prodigal.

Notions that Jesus became human, so that in him human beings might be adopted as children of God and be made heirs of God's kingdom, reflect a poverty of language—and imagination—in the face of mystery. The notion that Jesus the person lived before and beyond the birth of the child in Bethlehem opens Christianity to charges of polytheism unless one perceives that God's creative intention for the fullness of human being is, literally, as old as God. Thus, the birth of Jesus, like the creation of Adam—indeed, the birth of any child—marks a new genesis of God's intention for human being in a bodied person.

I find this possibility consonant with the Christian concept of vocation, opening us to a Jesus who was in every way as we are, yet did not sin—which is to say, a Jesus who was in every way as we are, yet perceived and responded to God's intention for a humanness as prodigally self-giving as God's own lavish generosity. To say that Jesus "became human," then, is an acknowledgment that even though one is born *homo sapiens*, born a human creature, to *become* human entails more than existence; to *become* human is a lifelong response shaped in and by love of God. In a lifelong vocation of becoming human, of being all that God intends for humans to be, Jesus reveals the fullness, the wholeness, the integrity of human being.

Moreover, the concept of adoption may convey something quite different, and far more encouraging, than a hasty or simplistic reading suggests. After all, the assertion of Genesis echoed in the first premise of the Christian creeds maintains that God is the maker of all things. Every child is, then, a child of God. But as children made and endowed with freedom, our relationship with God, and God's relationship with us, consists of more than progenitive necessity. If, in freedom, we are at liberty to choose or reject the God who made us, then is not God also at liberty to choose, or reject, us? In Jesus—in his person, his life, his responsive relationship with God—we perceive a God who *chooses* to love humanity, who *chooses* to love us.

Inheritance in the biblical cultures, as we know from the story of Jacob and Esau (Genesis 27) and from gospel parables (Mark 10; Luke 10 & 18), was based not only upon kinship, but on paternal affirmation. Remember again the practical realities of birth that substantiate the legitimacy of the mother but render fatherhood a matter of faith. A child's mother can be verified; until DNA testing, paternity was open to question. Therefore, in the biblical eras, inheritance required the father's blessing, the affirmation of choice. Jesus, in word and in the substance of his life, evidences that we are embraced by God, assured of our place in God's family.

The importance of Jesus' suffering and death is not that it affects but that it affirms God's intentions for human being. Jesus' vocation was to real-ize what it means to be fully human—by whatever means demanded.

The story *could* have ended differently. Jesus *did* devote himself to teaching, preaching, the practice of radical healing and hospitality—any and all of which might have sufficed to persuade us to a new and different perception of God, a deeper relationship with God as Jonah saw at Nineveh. But life and mission end differently. As he knelt in Gethsemane (Matthew 26; Mark 14) and faced into the terrifying reality of what might be required of him, he was caught between the rock of his trust in God and the hard place made for him by the unheeding and willful hardness of human hearts. The one thing demanded of his vocation was unconditional, disinterested love. In that moment he prays for strength to see beyond his own self-interest and welfare. Had one held a mirror before him and given him a glimpse of his own face, he would have known in that instant that he had truly become his Father.

If Jesus' suffering and death affect God, they surely and simultaneously broke and rejoiced God's heart. Jesus' self-giving affirms God's intentions for human being even as the circumstances confirm the cost of God's own gift of freedom—both are the consequence of prodigal love. Jesus' fulfillment of the vocation to real-ize what it means to be wholly human, by whatever means demanded, breaks the power of sin and reconciles humanity to God.

If sin is estrangement from God, and any barrier that prevents our drawing nearer to God, Jesus' life and death radically refute and forever challenge the excuse "I'm only human." In Jesus I am assured that to be only human is an invitation to divinity; I am assured that God is both hopelessly and hopefully in love with us humans, each of us, all of us.

That is the significance of Jesus' resurrection. We are fascinated by the reincarnational aspect of resurrection. Our preoccupation with that somewhat simplistic and superficial dimension obscures other considerations and connections that link this event with the larger narrative. Again, we need the *whole* story to appreciate what our ancestors in faith perceived and bequeathed to us. Recall that within Eden there stood two trees, the Tree of Knowledge and the Tree of Eternal Life. They are not told they shall never taste the fruit of the trees or share the harvest, only that they are not to presume to eat the fruit before it is given. When they exercise their freedom and pluck the fruit of the Tree of Knowledge, they get a big helping of knowledge, learning pretty quickly that freedom has consequences. They are expelled from the garden. No more fruit from the Tree of Knowledge (suggesting that if knowledge is proportional to rations, we humans have been functioning ever since on little more than a snack's worth).

But wait. There were *two* trees in the garden. There was also the Tree of Eternal Life. They were forbidden to eat of *both*, for if they ate of both they would die, said God. Interestingly, in every place God forbids them to eat of the trees, the rationale is that eating would result in death—which could have meant little to people and a place as yet untouched by death. Adam and Eve do not even possess sufficient knowledge or awareness to ask for a definition of terms. It's the serpent who leverages their handicap and introduces the more tempting rationale: that eating would result in their becoming like God. Both rationales are likely correct; the one thing the rationales have in common is that eating would result in Adam and Eve becoming something *other* than what and who God intended them to be.

The stories of the two Adams is stunning for its symmetries. The old Adam is born to, inhabits, and is eventually expelled from a garden. The new Adam, Jesus, is betrayed, buried, and resurrected in a garden. The old Adam is nailed by a tree, the new Adam nailed to a tree. The old Adam is denied the fruit Eternal Life; the new Adam, Jesus, offers to all the first fruits of the same. Not just to some, but to all. Not just to the living, but to the dead, for none shall be denied God's love.

Yet to see only the revivification of Jesus' body is to miss much. The resurrection of Jesus, regardless the details of the phenomenon, is the only and most poignantly powerful symbol adequate to convey the true nature of the God of self-giving, prodigal love. It is the tangible expression of the triumph of love over justice. Or perhaps it is more prudent to say that it is the incarnate expression of a love and a justice so far surpassing all human notions of either as to be only of God.

What human father, suffering the cruel rejection and brutal execution of his child, could be so generous? Such justice as we know is informed by and based only upon a bite of the Tree of Knowledge; by our cramped, crabbed notions of justice, death demands recompense in death. Our justice is still bounded by self-regard, self-interest. Our justice demands requital; every love deserves an equal love, every hurt demands an equal hurt. By any measure of our justice, the death of Jesus cries out to be avenged. Yet those who knew Jesus, who experienced Jesus, were persuaded differently.

Whenever he came to them, however he came to them, the stories they told and recorded point to a new and different way. In nearly every instance, the resurrected Jesus greets them with assurance, counsels them "do not be afraid." It's a direct address to their natural, human instinct that demands recompense for his innocent death. He is at pains to restore, instill trust.

He ascended into heaven, they maintained, and is seated at the right hand of the Father. Jesus took our human nature into heaven, reigns with God and intercedes for us. In these boldly imaginative claims the reunion of God's intent with earth's reality is consummated. The "only" Son of God to perfectly fulfill God's intention for humankind returns to the source of all life. Though hampered by the insufficiencies of language and limited to the constructs of human order, despite the spatial problems posed by ascent, heaven, reign, and intercession, these assertions are breathtaking in their scope and mildly amusing in their craft.

They are breathtaking, too, in what they proclaim of human nature. Nineteenth-century Anglican priest and poet Christopher Wordsworth gives expression to this audacity in a hymn in which he declares that the ascended Jesus "Hast raised our human nature on the clouds to God's right hand: there we sit in heavenly places, there with (Jesus) in glory stand. / Jesus reigns, adored by angels; Man with God is on the throne; mighty Lord, in thine ascension, we by faith behold our own" (*The Hymnal 1982*, #215).

The image of Jesus as intercessor in a court setting is less appealing, and perhaps even deficient without an appreciation of Jesus as a counterbalance to the rainbow over Noah on Ararat. In the earlier story of God's anger and the ensuing deluge, God set a rainbow in the sky, not so much as an assurance to Noah, but as a reminder to God. At the sight of the rainbow God would recall the promise made never again to destroy the people. The presence of Jesus at the right hand of God, the right hand being the position reserved for help, suggests that the ascended Jesus occupies the place reserved for the co-creator—the role bestowed upon humankind at creation. But like the rainbow, the eternal presence of Jesus also serves to keep ever before God this incarnation of humanness, "helps" God remember the fullness of God's intent for each of us.

How do we share the life, the humanity, fulfilled in Jesus? How do we participate in relationship with God, preserving our humanity while realizing our divinity? How do we become whole, fully real-ized human beings, fulfilling our own vocations as persons of genuine integrity? As an old aphorism maintains, the longest journey begins with a single step. To share the relationship with God manifested in Jesus, we assent to seek and enter a new relationship with God, a relationship radically, fundamentally different—a relationship of prodigal disinterested self-giving.

10

A New Kind of Relationship

EW ASPECTS of Christianity are as potentially harmful to human relations as the notion of a "new" covenant. This may be partly the result of our tendency to invest the word *new* with connotations of superiority. But at core, *new* means only "different" and, in reference to time, "more recent." In this sense, while a "new" thing may indeed be novel or unique, in the matter of relationship God, "new" presumes a preexisting reality; the "new" covenant is not so much unique or novel as it is "different from" the kind of relationship that went before.

All living relationships grow, thus all living relationships are being constantly made new. This is one of the exciting dynamics of relationship. Yet while a living relationship is new every day, the essence—the core—of the relationship, the basic commitment of one person to another, remains the same. The notion that Jesus supplants the original relationship between God and humans established at creation and renewed through Noah, Abraham, and all their descendants, is challenged by Jesus himself. Jesus on many occasions denied that he had come to abolish or replace that original relationship. His vocation, as he expressed it, was to fulfill that relationship.

That is not to say that Jesus' vocation was in any way to "finish" the relationship between God and humankind. The fulfillment of relationship is not the end of relationship, but rather the highest realization of relationship. Throughout the history of relationship between God and humanity there have been those who found within the model of human sexual intimacy an analogue for a fulfilled relationship with God.

The deepest human longing, the urge and desire to know and be known to and by another, emerges frequently from the pages of scripture. The ancient Hebrew word for sexual intercourse is most accurately translated in English as "to know." "To know" someone, in the biblical sense, was and is to share the profound union of sexual congress, the most intimate joining of two bodies. The Song of Songs is unabashedly graphic, and profoundly modern, in its descriptions of this deep and powerful bonding as the ultimate expression of relationship with God.

The model of human sexual intimacy reverberates through the written history of our faith, surfacing time and again in the writings of saints and mystics. Theresa of Avila, among others, perceived relationship with God in highly charged sexual images, these encounters equivalent to the richest union of lovers. Despite periodic retreats into prudery which, when set within the larger context of history prove to be the perverted exceptions, these powerful sexual images persist as icons of perfect love between God and humankind.

Is this not consistent with the gradual progression in relationship deemed wisdom by generations of human experience? Why shouldn't the primary relationship of our human lives—one's relationship to God, the ultimate Being and ultimate Other—conform to patterns of human relating that call us to progress from self-centered isolation to the ultimate giving of oneself to another?

Furthermore, if we read biblical scriptures as the record of a gradually unfolding story of relationship between God and humanity, a relationship that moves through varied experiences and trials, each leading to closer and deeper union between the partners at the core of the story, we understand more clearly how such a relationship might be expected to eventuate in the ultimate union of those partners.

Be mindful, however, that all human analogies are flawed and incomplete. As the apostle Paul noted, our relationship with God is a treasured mystery we attempt to convey in fragile earthen vessels (2 Corinthians 4:7). If and when we carry the sexual imagery too far, the pottery cracks and shatters.

For example, if we follow the analogy of God as parent, then sexual images tangle us hopelessly in incest. And if we get carried away with analogies based on sexual intercourse, we contrive all manner of problems for ourselves. Suffice it to say, the urge to relationship with God, like our urge for human relationship, is based on a deep and profoundly mysterious desire, even need—to give, to be received/accepted and to receive. Such powerful giving and receiving in mutuality are arrived at only gradually in any relationship and, when met, mark a *new* kind of relationship. As the potent experience of sexual love teaches each of us, in the dawn of "the morning after" one realizes that a threshold has been crossed; a new kind of commitment is in the offing.

Growth into, and movement toward, this kind of intimate mutuality is learned; we are socialized into our relationships. Many of us learn about intimate mutuality in homes where this profound mystery is experienced in our parents. To see and experience the possibility, to be surrounded by the potential of such relationship, is one step toward this growth. But a rather common example serves to suggest how we pass eventually from possibility to our own potent reality in relationship.

As a schoolboy I sometimes found myself in awe of a more popular student, or of one whose talents I admired. Even today there are those I admire from afar—the author of a favorite book, the occasional celebrity, public leader, or intellectual. Occasionally, I might learn that one of my own friends or acquaintances enjoyed a close relationship with this person I perceived to be unapproachable. I have sometimes been relieved when that friend, sensing my interest or apprehension, initiated an introduction and established a new relationship between me and the person I had feared to approach. My joy is complete when such relationships eventuate in a genuinely mutual respect and affection, when all three of us in this new relationship find a new kind of being with one another.

This homely example helps me comprehend how the "New Covenant" at the heart of the Christian life constitutes a new relationship with God imparted by Jesus to the apostles and, through them, to successive generations who believe in and share their relationship with him. This simple social pattern by which circles of relationship are extended and enlarged seem to me the very model of what Christians have historically defined as "evangelism." In fact, it seems a major oversight to deny Jesus the title "evangelist," for who is more deserving than the one who bore in himself the good news of God's love for us?

It has always been "good news" to me to see and learn that one from whom I felt distant and even inferior was, indeed, approachable—that this person was not only approachable, but desired, enjoyed, and valued me and my friendship. This "good news" is greatly magnified when the One from whom I feel distant and inferior is God.

In and through Jesus—in the relationship Jesus seems to have shared with God, in what Jesus perceived of God and in the rich trust Jesus evidenced in God—I am encouraged to draw near to God. I persist in my appreciation of Jesus' humanity precisely because it keeps me near God; Jesus' insistence in his own "ordinariness," that he is and was "in every way as we are," as I am, binds me in my relationship with God.

Might one have a relationship with God without Jesus? Certainly. At a profound level, I (and presumably all Christians) have a relationship with God quite apart from the relationship with Jesus; Jesus himself was quite clear about the distinction between himself and God. But *my* experience, my reality is a relationship with God that includes Jesus. To return to my analogy, while I might eventually develop a deep and even intimate relationship with a person to whom I am introduced by a mutual friend—which is often the case of our most intimate relationships—if I value that intimate relationship, I also value and honor the loving friend to whom I owe that relationship. And while there is a distinction in the nature of each relationship, true mutuality insists that each is profoundly bound to the other.

Clarity and honesty demand that I confess that it is not merely upon the word of Jesus that I am persuaded to risk relationship with God. I am encouraged not only by what Jesus may have said of God, but also by what I see evidenced in the relationship between Jesus and God. Most of us know the disjuncture between word and reality; a wife may insist that her husband is loving, yet the bruises on her face say differently. Conversely, we also know that the conjunction of word and reality creates a powerful and palpable perception transcending language alone; the poise and assurance of the person who knows himself or herself to be genuinely, truly loved and respected is evidenced in them. Jesus didn't have to *say* that God is love; Jesus lived in the deepest and most abiding awareness of that love. As the most poetic gospel expresses it, that love was so pervasively and potently manifest in him that were all human tongues silenced, "the stones would shout out" (Luke 19:40). It is that potent expression of this reality manifested in him that distinguishes Jesus the person from "the Christ"—the one in whom word alone is transcended, the one in whom the fullness of human being and divine love meet and are manifested. Thus when the church speaks of "the Christ" it understands this designation as "the total package."

In this way we acknowledge that relationship with God is neither predicated nor ventured upon intellectual argument and assent. I'm not encouraged to draw closer to and enter into relationship with God simply because Jesus told his friends and companions that it was okay; we've learned a *few* things since Eden. That was how the serpent prevailed; on his word alone. Moreover, the serpent didn't take a preliminary bite of the fruit, nothing that might instill confidence in the promised outcome. I am encouraged, indeed I deeply, profoundly love God and am deeply, profoundly loved by God because Jesus' own prior relationship with God persuades me of this reality.

The promise in the New Covenant is not, then, mere assurance. When Jesus promises to bring us into the kingdom of God and give us life in all its fullness this is not an anticipatory assurance. "Promise" is more than a pledge anticipating fulfillment; there is another, and more elemental, definition of *promise* derived from the Latin *pro-* + *mittere*, meaning literally "to send forth." A promise is a declaration not only that one will do something specified but is the performance of the same. Thus, to enter into relationship with God as Jesus is in relationship with God *is* to enter God's realm—God's reality—and to experience, to possess, to embrace life in all its fullness.

Engagement of any relationship and entry into mutuality is always a response. I have never truly initiated any relationship. I don't have it in me to do so. That's not to say that I'm antisocial. It's only to acknowledge my dependency. I did not birth myself. Nor have I made any part of this world. I acknowledge that it all has its genesis in God. Therefore every relationship in my life—good, bad, or indifferent—is a response to God's prior gift.

This is an essential acknowledgment when engaging those teachings of the church that treat the matter of what Christ "requires" or "commands." Neither word is wholly satisfactory to convey the dynamic of response in relationship. Requirement and commandment connote rules, a conditional contract. A relationship established upon love, especially the love of a prodigal God who loves us even before we are aware of that love, seems careless of rules, unheeding of requirement. So how am I to understand this seeming contradiction?

All life is bounded; when we assign a word to anything, we are attempting to establish boundaries that give that thing shape, that allow us to frame our perceptions of that thing, and to share those perspectives with others. My skin, my body, represent the boundary of my mortal person. This person was given a name at birth, and a little bracelet whose beads spelled out that name so that my tiny little bounded being wouldn't be mistaken for someone else. When I was baptized, that name was conferred as my "Christian" name, the name by which my little bounded being was identified before God. In carrying out this exercise, my parents were repeating the first work of Adam, simply naming a creature they believed to be the handiwork and gift of God. Not that God needed my name, any more than God cared whether that creature with the long neck was called giraffe, or the squishy thing gliding through the ocean depths be called squid. But relationship demands names, designation of the other. Thus we might properly say that the reality of a varied creation filled with different creatures *required* names by which each could be honored for its uniqueness.

Encouraged to relationship with God by what I apprehend and perceive in Jesus the Christ, as I draw near, enter, and mature into that relationship, I am in a constant, perpetual state of response. Even the choice to withhold or deny response is a response—that's the ironic predicament of the atheist, whose posture of denial presupposes some*thing* to deny. Indeed, I and countless others have persisted in resisting the prodigal love of God, and successfully, for God will not force my response. Remember, the prodigal God loves without requital; God's love in no way depends upon my loving in return. I cannot stop God loving me any more than I can stop another person's loving, or hating, me; I am not granted control over the emotions of others, no matter how much I might wish that control, or convince myself than I am capable of it.

But the gradual and growing awareness of God's love for me encourages me to assent to that love. Once I accept the love God holds out to me, once I step into the circle of relationship into which Jesus the Christ invites me, I become aware simultaneously of my desire to love in response, and my own inexperience in such loving.

I have been gravely insecure; the circumstances of my life, despite (or perhaps even because of) relative privilege and a loving family, instilled within me a deep fear of rejection. For most of my childhood and youth I felt pretty unlovable. I was physically awkward, was bookish and artistic in a social culture that deemed such qualities effete. Consequently, young adulthood was for me a succession of hopeless infatuations, a pit of bottomless neediness. I threw myself at anyone who evidenced the slightest appreciation or affection for me. The ensuing assault was usually devastatingly fatal, killing the tender shoots of love before they could possibly take root. In other words, I had not yet learned how to love.

God and I had an abortive fling when I was in late adolescence, a time when most of us are prone to excesses of hormones and emotion. One warm evening in Shady Grove Methodist Church, after a rousing revivalist's sermon and one too many verses of "Just As I Am," my chubby, acne-pocked self made a tearful path to the altar rail, knelt, and vowed to accept Jesus as my personal Lord and Savior. Thereafter followed the predictable trajectory of infatuation. I plunged into an orgy of Bible reading, prayer, and superficial holiness—enough to smother even the God of Abraham.

What I failed to see is that this ill-formed immaturity was, at bottom, all about me. I wasn't truly receiving, or rejoicing in, God's love for me. I was still trying to win love, earn love. It had not yet come to me that God neither "required" nor "commanded" anything of me. God simply loves me.

What, then, does it mean to my life that God loves me? What does the shape of such love take? First and foremost, the love manifest in the Christ is based upon no more and nothing less than trust— ultimate and profound trust—in the prodigal, unconditional love of God. In other words, if we wish to enter the relationship, we have only to begin where Jesus begins: profound trust in the reality of God's prodigal love for him, for each of us, for *me*.

The relationship with God we see and know in the Christ is distinguished from and shaped by identifiable characteristics. When pressed to articulate those characteristics, Jesus did not resort to invention. Rather, he repeated the wisdom inherited from successive generations of other human beings who, before him, had encountered and embraced the love of God: those who truly trust and embrace the love God has for them shall, in response, love the Lord God with all their heart, with all their soul, and with all their mind. This is the first and great compulsion of the genuine love of God and human met in the Christ. And the second is like it: those who truly trust and embrace the love God has for them shall, in response, love their neighbor as they love themselves.

Therein lay the secret of my earlier undoing; I did not, could not, accept or trust God's love for me, nor could I truly respond to that love, until I grew in love for myself. There, too, lies one of the most serious shortcomings of much Christian teaching. Not only does some Christian teaching counsel an inordinate lack of self-regard by enforcing an unthinking self-abnegation, but further compounds that dereliction in the false assumptions of instantaneous conversion. While it is certainly possible that an exceptional person might fall deeply, profoundly, and maturely in love with another person, the more usual human experience is a pretty clumsy succession of haphazard relationships of varying intensity, duration, and damage. In other words, we only gradually grow into love—with one another, and with God. Just as I did not live happily ever after in undying affection with the first person for whom I felt a crushing rush of love at the age of five, neither did I arise from the revivalist's altar call to find myself ensconced in a fully formed, mature relationship with God.

That one might experience such a profound trust so quickly, and respond appropriately, may well be possible, but it accords neither with my experience nor that of most of the family of God whose stories are recorded in scripture. If, as Christians believe and teach, the shape of genuine love for God is that we love one another as Christ loved us, then this process is the work and span of a lifetime, and perhaps beyond. Like every relationship, it is a journey, each traveler's path, perspective, and experience unique.

But it is not a sojourn without documentation. All the great religions of human history possess the historical logs of the collective journey, the diaries of relationship, some intensely personal, others quite public and political, which is to say, shaped by the times and cultures of their making. For Christians, some of the journey is recorded in the biblical scriptures, and summarized in the creeds.

11

Necessity Is the
Mother of Invention

ECHNICALLY, A CREED is any statement of belief. Very
early and elemental articulations of belief are scattered
throughout the biblical books. One of the oldest is Israel's
declaration that their God is distinct from others' gods: "Hear O
Israel, the Lord is our God, the Lord alone" (Deuteronomy 6:4), a formula that persists and reappears, as in the First Book of Kings: ". . . all
the people . . . fell on their faces; and they said, 'The Lord, he is God;
the Lord, he is God'"(18:39).

In the Christian scriptures these statements are often personal,
profound utterances of insight and conviction spoken by and identified with specific characters, like Peter's response to Jesus' question
"Who do you say that I am?": "You are the Christ, the Son of the
living God" (Matthew 16:16), and Thomas's shocked reaction to the
resurrected Jesus standing before him offering evidence of the crucifixion in wounded hands: "My Lord and my God!" (John 20:28).
Or the words of the apostle Paul to the Christians gathered in
Corinth, divided among themselves and in need of some basics from
which they might derive healing and unity: ". . . for us there is one

God, the Father, from whom are all things and for whom we exist, and one Lord, Jesus Christ, through whom are all things and through whom we exist" (1 Corinthians 8:6) and ". . . I delivered to you as of first importance what I also received, that Christ died for our sins in accordance with the scriptures, that he was buried, that he was raised on the third day in accordance with the scriptures, and that he appeared to Cephas, then to the twelve" (1 Corinthians 15:3–5).

The creeds of the Christian church are among the more curious and complex features of its life. Of the numerous creeds produced, the Nicene Creed and the Apostles' Creed are most commonly met in modern worship; the Athanasian Creed remains a feature in some liturgies, most notably on Trinity Sunday. No one set out to produce these documents for sheer creative exercise. Each was drafted, and crafted, in times and under circumstances of acute crisis within the believing community. From the outset of human history opinions, perspectives, and beliefs have been as numerous as the people who hold them. For long stretches of time the church has endured with minimal concern for the varieties of opinion, perspective, and belief. But occasionally there has arisen so much contention that a sorting and ordering seemed a necessity.

The Apostles' Creed, though traditionally linked to those whose name it bears, probably owes its composition largely to the late second and early third centuries; the earliest known text dates to around 215. Earlier first-centuries texts in scripture, including the gospels, Acts, and nearly every epistle, evidence that distinct communities of believers in the Christ were already formed, and openly disagreed on fundamentals of the faith. It is hardly surprising that after some two hundred or more years matters reached a point begging for consultation and clarity.

Four hundred, five hundred years after the birth and death of Jesus, communities of Christian learning and worship had grown and become integrated into the social and political cultures of their times, fostering a lively life and the friction that comes of diversity and power. Councils throughout this period convened to debate and determine the shape of the *dominant* faith. Those whose arguments prevailed in the Council at Nicea in 325 and at Constantinople in 381 bequeathed us the Nicene Creed.

Although the Athanasian Creed bears the name of an early church scholar named Athanasius who lived in the late fourth century (around 370), it is now held more likely that the text was developed in the fifth or sixth century. Thus it would seem that a periodic review arose with some regularity, and communities of believers revisited and reiterated the principles they held to be fundamental.

Like other "boundaries" described previously, the basic principles articulated in a creed define the basis for a faith community's identity, its perception of itself, and its presentation of itself to the world of which it is only a part. It is interesting, instructive, and humbling to note that none of the classic creeds of the Christian faith were necessitated by confusion or conflict with other religionists, nonbelievers, or pagans. Each was precipitated by conflict and confusion *among* Christians themselves, and each was formulated to establish distinct boundaries around the institutional community called the church by articulating the essential fundaments of the faith.

As statements of basic beliefs about God, the creeds are both a beginning point and a periodic resting place for the journey of faith; we begin with such basics and return to them when we need reorienting. Yet, like all the instruments of religion, a creed is only a means to an end, and not the end in itself; to place *anything* above God, who is the ultimate destination of our sojourn, is always idolatry.

The familiar Nicene and Apostles' creeds begin with the affirmation, we (or I) *believe*. The operative word is *believe*. Believing is not the same as knowing. Believing begins where knowing ends, which, I find as I grow older, is a place I encounter with alarming and increasing frequency. On the road to God, along the route of my life, the pavement of knowledge often comes to an abrupt halt and I can venture forward only on what I believe. When that happens, I must risk.

Years ago I made a retreat with a group of students to a favorite spot nestled in the Blue Ridge Mountains of North Carolina. On our last evening, we spent a quiet evening by a fireplace, and retired to deep sleep aided by the sound of rain. The next morning we stood on the porch of our cabin and surveyed the valley below, which overnight had become the oversized bed of a swirling river the color of chocolate milk. Hastening to make a long drive home, we loaded our cars and set out. At the bottom of the mountain, we came to a spot in the road where a small bridge spanned what had been, only hours earlier, a trickling brook. The rails of the bridge were still visible, but the bed was not. Contrary to all wisdom, I affirmed my belief in the unseen by backing the car up slightly, revving the engine, and rushing across the divide. We were fortunate; the bridge was still there.

A few miles farther along the journey, we were stopped in a long line of cars. Exiting the car and walking around the bend, we stood in awe at the sight of nearly two hundred yards of pavement neatly excised from the route and now resting at the bottom of a ravine, sheared from the mountainside by a torrent. As we made our way more cautiously by an alternate route, I was all the more aware of the tremendous risk I had taken with my welfare and the lives of others entrusted to me.

That experience remains in memory and returns every second of every day in a new guise, at every point where the road of my knowledge abruptly ends and I must proceed in faith. At the rain-swollen stream I had literally bet my life—and the lives of others—that a bridge was still there, that its deck was still intact, that we'd make it across.

That's faith: to bet one's life, to risk all that one is and all that one has. Everyone has faith. Make no mistake about it; every one of us lives every day on assumptions, most of them uninformed, not just because of indolence and willful ignorance—of which there's plenty—but because there are limits to what any of us *can* know. And those assumptions shape every decision, determine all outcomes.

As a Christian, I subscribe to the fundamental principle articulated in the first affirmation of the Apostles' and Nicene creeds: I believe in God, the creator of heaven and earth, maker of all things visible and invisible. If I believed only that, it would suffice. If I allowed that fundamental principle to inform my every decision, to illuminate every consideration and motivate every act, it would be sufficient. For I would then honor God in receiving everything not only as God's gift to me, but as a gift related to me by birth in God, radically connected to me in some fundamental way.

But I also subscribe to the affirmations that embrace the story of Jesus. For me these affirmations are not essentials so much as they are specifiers. That is to say that they "frame" my essential affirmation of the one, unitive, creative God. They establish the basis, the route, by which I come to the primary and, for me, unshakable affirmation articulated in the first principle of the creed.

Such contextual or circumstantial elements are often a part of one's creed. We're a people of stories. For me, the story undergirding my faith in the one God who made all that is, seen and unseen, is the story of the Christ. Our Hebrew ancestors based their faith in the same God upon another story:

> A wandering Aramean was my ancestor; he went down into Egypt, and lived there as an alien, few in number, and there he became a great nation, mighty and populous. When the Egyptians treated us harshly and afflicted us, by imposing hard labor upon us, we cried to the LORD, the God of our ancestors; the LORD heard our voice and saw our affliction, our toil, and our oppression. The LORD brought us forth out of Egypt with a mighty hand and an outstretched arm, with a terrifying display of power, and with signs and with wonders; and he brought us into this place, and gave us this land, a land flowing with milk and honey. (Deuteronomy 26:5–9)

Our Jewish sisters and brothers trace their faith in God to this ancestral story, which for them continues to define their contemporary experience. Imagine the impact and the import of this story for a modern generation of survivors of Auschwitz, Treblinka, and Dachau. The currency of the story to their experience continues to inform and shape their faith.

I come to faith in the same God by way of a different story, the story of a child born homeless in Bethlehem, innocently and mercilessly crucified, yet alive to friends only three days later—alive to me, whom he calls "friend" even today. The distinctive quality of both stories is that each is firmly rooted in the documentable history of our human experience, inseparable from our bounded realm of time and space; yet each is also contemporary, a living story whose trajectory transcends both time and space, whose embrace is universal. This transcendence is not mere artful contrivance. It is mystery. And when properly imparted, when shared as story, each of these tales is genuinely universal, touching common human experiences that transcend the narrow boundaries of Judaism or Christianity.

The stories are universal; the religions, sadly, are not. Once the stories were appropriated as essential elements of faith, taken up into creeds, they ceased to function as unifying instruments of a God who in both Hebrew (Old Testament) and Christian (New Testament) scriptures is perceived and portrayed as a God who wills to bring all into union. The stories ceased to be embracing stories of universal human experience that brought all who shared them to common ground and became, instead, specific conditions for membership in a tribal, bounded faith community. In framing the stories as conditions of faith, as essential principles, instead of honoring the stories as the descriptive experiences and contexts within which the believer has come to trust God, by which the believer abides in faith, the stories are treated not as the bountiful gift of a prodigally generous God, but as property owned and controlled by particular groups within the larger human family.

To see the story of the Christ reduced to a skeletal outline, as it is in the creeds, may be helpful to me and those within my own faith community as an abbreviated recitation of my faith journey, but to impose that outline as essential to faith in the one God does grave injustice to the story itself. The story begs to be told, to be shared and savored, to be amplified, not abbreviated; the story invites *my* story, encourages me to enter and engage the *spirit* of all story. For all story is relational. Every story depends upon both a teller and a hearer. Every story invites relationship. When we reduce the story to outline and codify it as conditional to faith, we kill the spirit.

Christianity and Judaism are profoundly relational religions, as the stories underlying our creeds reveal. The great struggle of religions is the difficulty of mediating mystery: How does one give expression to the ineffable? How does one *realize*—literally *make real*—relationship with the invisible God? Every human contrivance falls short. Every medium available to us in time and space is limited; whether we use gold, silver, stone or words, ideas and images, we eventually end in idolatry—which is clearly and wisely forbidden. Christian religion is relational. The struggle to articulate the foundational relationality at the heart of Christianity gave rise to this religion's most controversial doctrine: the Trinity.

The Trinity is both mystery and metaphor, and each should give us pause. The mystery should encourage us to humility. The metaphor should encourage us to prudence, lest we confuse our doctrinal imaginings with material realities and end in idolatry. But as paradigm of relationship, I still find the Trinity helpful in my attempt to embrace the God who so diligently seeks and embraces me, the one God described in three dimensions: Father, Son, and Holy Spirit.

Just as the authors of Genesis "work backwards," attempting to make sense and meaning out of the world as they receive it, so the authors of the Trinity have attempted to make sense and meaning of God as they have received God. Despite the considerable limitations and weaknesses of both Genesis and the doctrine of the Trinity, each is worthy of respect and appreciation for the assistance they provide us in our own apprehension of reality. Genesis begins the written history of a people whose experience of the world led them to discern the work of a single and generous Being in whose creativity everything finds both origin and unity. That history continues in numerous books relating the growth of relationship between God and creation.

The Trinity offers an imaginative discernment of the relationship between God and creation. Denied material access to this God who is mysteriously omnipresent while maddeningly incorporeal, the genius and wisdom of the Trinity is that it allows us a three-dimensional God yet does not infringe the prohibition of idolatry. Our God is met and known in three spatial and temporal dimensions.

Our God is met in the creative generativity of a father who, because a father's life predates that of his offspring, is of the past, is historical. Our God is met in the life of a son whose birth allows both father and child to be contemporaries, both sharing the present. That Father is the one whom we call God and know as the maker of all things, who called Abraham and Sarah to particular vocation and established a relationship with them and their descendants. That Son is the one whom we call Jesus and know as the human being called to the fullness of God's intention for humankind and consecrated as the Christ in his fulfillment of that vocation. This singular God and this paradigmatic human son whose life literally incorporates the will of God for all human life are yet only two dimensions of a God who is still more. Our God is a living God met and known in the fullness of relationship, met and known in spirit.

12

One in the Spirit

HE HOLY SPIRIT is traditionally defined as the Third Person of the Trinity, the other two persons being the Father and the Son. One of the most troublesome difficulties of the Trinity is this word *person*. In its Latin origin, the word means "mask." It's the word that describes the actor's role, the *persona*. It's a difficult word to employ in imaginative discourse because it is so deeply associated with human being. Thus, when we hear or speak the word, we have in mind the kind of being we are: sensing, thinking, bodily creatures. The difficulty is further complicated by the lack of any other word that might adequately substitute; no matter the word we choose, limitations intervene—like the three-legged dog.

That being said, I venture that "person" can be understood as a much larger word than we commonly allow. When we consider its roots in ancient theater, we see that "person" is more than just the creaturely being; it includes also the "role" fulfilled in that human being. Right away we see that this word has rich complexities and huge capacities, for the actor is a single being with the potential for many roles. Yet we understand that no matter the role the actor may inhabit at the moment, all the roles and the being must be considered as a whole to really honor what we mean when we speak of this *person*. For example, I have seen Robin Williams inhabit the roles of Patch Adams and Mrs. Doubtfire and a host of other weird and wonderful characters. I also know that Robin Williams is a father whose children attend a school whose headmaster is an old friend of mine. Thus when I think or speak of Robin Williams I include those aspects and more. To maintain that Robin Williams is only the actor in the role of Mrs. Doubtfire, or only the father at the PTA meeting, is to discount (and dishonor) the wholeness of this person.

In the matter of the Trinity, each of the "persons" is every bit as complex (and sometimes as funny) as Robin Williams. Or you and me. Is it so difficult or strange to conceive of God as a being whose fullness, whose wholeness incorporate multiple persons, roles, or aspects? After all, every man and woman is someone's child; each may be partner or spouse; some may be a parent. Yet each is always himself, herself. One in many and many in one. None of us appreciates being reduced to a role, or thought of in terms of a single aspect. We are rightly offended to be treated as less than a whole.

The Holy Spirit seems to me a natural and logical consequence of relationship. Every relationship between two persons is trinitarian. When you and I share a relationship, I remain me and you remain you. Yet, in addition to me and you, there is also that "who" we are together, that elusive but very real and sometimes palpable person made of the union between us. My parents afford a handy example for me.

My father and mother are quite different people, each with a unique history and very particular gifts and traits. I know each of them, and have had very different relationships with each of them; indeed, one profound dimension of this difference lies in the fact that as I write this, my father lives and my mother has died, but I am still in relationship to each. Despite their singular individuality, in their love for one another and the relationship in which they live, I am profoundly aware of a third person—the "who" they are together. Proceeding from their relationship, this third "person" has a history, a life, and a power I cannot deny. As much as either of them, this spirit proceeding from their shared life has shaped me, my siblings, and the entire world inhabited by us all.

I have emphasized the distinct characters of God and humankind. I have described the singular relationship between God and the archetypal, paradigmatic human being named Jesus, in whose vocation and life all the faith, love, and hope of God for humankind are realized and consecrated, entitling Jesus to bear the name "Christ." Of this deep and abiding relationship of God and Jesus is born the Holy Spirit, that powerful spirit arising from and enfolding this powerful, prodigal love of each for the other. God's love for humankind and Jesus' love for God are each irrational; neither conforms to our human, rational definition or expectations of love. Each is selfless, and generous to a fault. Out of so powerful and prodigal a love an abundant stream flows, and sweeps us up in its refreshing, restorative waters.

Of this love, the Holy Spirit is revealed in the Old Covenant as the giver of life, the One who spoke through the prophets. Of this love, the Holy Spirit is revealed as the Lord who leads us into all truth and enables us to grow in the likeness of Christ. Of this love, the Holy Spirit is revealed in us, in our own time and the space of our lives, when we are in love and harmony with God, with ourselves, with our neighbors, and with all creation.

But how do we know we are truly in love and harmony with God, with ourselves, with our neighbors, and with all creation? I'm easily deluded into a false sense of security. My world, large as it is, is still a bounded sphere, and so small in comparison to "all creation." Is the love and harmony sought by God measured in my own meager attempts at affection, my little acts of kindness and charity? Is it enough that I simply feel good about myself, am content with my feelings toward God, self, and neighbor? How do I distinguish between a complacency and happiness manufactured out of my own will and disciplines, and the genuine love compelled by the power of the Spirit that proceeds from God's love in Christ, Christ's love in God?

The short and honest answer is, we can't know. Remember, that's what distinguishes faith from knowledge in all relationships. Our status in relationship is always a matter of trust. But we are not completely rudderless. We're not flying blind. We're inheritors of a long experience, and all the wisdom that comes of experience, multiplied many times over by successive generations whose experience in relationship with God has bequeathed to us a rich repository of scripture, the chief anthology of which is that book we call the Bible.

The Bible is an anthology, a collection of over sixty books divided into two or three collections bound in a single volume. The Hebrew scriptures, sometimes called the Old Testament, comprise the first collection and consist of books written by the people of the Old Covenant, the covenant established by God with Abraham. These books are *inspired* by the Holy Spirit, literally created and animated by the Spirit proceeding from the relationship of God and his beloved humanity. Which is to say, these books were not written for gain or commerce, but for sheer love. These are journals of a people's love affair with God, and of God's love in return.

The Christian scriptures, sometimes called the New Testament, are a collection of books written by the people of the New Covenant, the covenant established by God in the Christ. These books, too, are inspired by the Holy Spirit, created and animated by the Spirit manifest in the relationship of God for all people in and through the Christ. They tell the story of the life and teachings of Jesus in four very different and sometimes contradictory gospels gathered, wisely, perhaps to remind us that while four very different people may live with and love the same person, each of their experiences of that person is uniquely theirs.

I am the eldest of five children who were privileged to grow to adulthood in the same household with the same parents. Yet each of us has different opinions of our parents based on our particular experiences. Over a decade experience separates my perceptions of my parents from that of my youngest sister; I encountered them first as newlyweds, my dad struggling to recover from a near-fatal illness and to complete a college degree, my mother learning to be a mother for the first time. My youngest sister encountered them as seasoned parents, nearing middle age, and unencumbered by a mortgage. Had all five of us set down our memoirs, many stories of our parents would emerge nearly identical, while some would be a complete surprise. And even the five memoirs would not sufficiently convey the entirety of our parents, whose lives were so much larger than the circle of our family. To draw even a cursory picture of either parent, one would need all the stories of a lifetime, and more, since the anticipation of their births no doubt affected the lives of those who came before them, even as the influence of each, and of the two of them together, will continue to shape our lives after their deaths.

The four gospels offer the foundational story with sufficient variety to preclude our tendencies to and pretensions of certainty, and encouragement to reflect upon and tell our own stories of the Christ whose presence we continue to know in our lives. But the four gospels also convey the Good News of God's love for all people interpreted in and derived from that story. Despite their different perspectives, each of the gospels agrees with the central principle of the predecessor stories in the Hebrew scriptures: that God made everything, and is madly in love with it all, most especially us humans. And despite our fickle foolishness, and our willful infidelities, God persists in this love, patient to love till love alone remains.

The books gathered in the Christian scriptures also tell the story of the power of that Good News to draw each of us in closer love for and with one another, and of the very real difficulties encountered even in love among people of good intention and faith. This is the story of the church at its beginning, recorded in the Acts of the Apostles and in the several letters exchanged among early communities of faith.

The Apocrypha is a collection of additional books of Hebrew scripture whose contents add nothing substantively different or new, but do amplify and often enliven stories contained within the Hebrew scriptures of the Old Testament. They are used by some in the Christian church to enrich our understanding and enjoyment.

The Holy Scriptures are called the Word of God, not because God dictated or delivered them. Rather, they are called the Word of God because they are accepted by the communities who gathered them and hold them close to be the product of relationship with God and, as such, are inspired—literally, have breath blown into them, derive their life—from this relationship. They are recognized not as the only texts inspired by this relationship, for indeed, every human carries such a story within, but they are recognized as the best representatives out of their generations. They are accorded this stature not simply for their art, but for their accessibility; their human authors and the experiences they share find affinity with our own lives and experiences; they touch the universal human experience and invite each of us to enter and engage God. They are remarkably generous and unpossessive; they are truly hospitable, and because they are so little compromised by the egos of their human authors, God still speaks to us through them.

Still, our understanding of the Bible is not unmediated. Despite the many excellent qualities of the biblical scriptures, each book therein has been touched by human hands; the original documents, their subsequent copies, additions, and subtractions, the variables of translation and the vagaries of the processes by which each was authenticated and chosen for inclusion in the final collection as we receive it all entailed human interaction. Since we believe that all human action includes not just the possibility but the probability of sin—that our tendencies toward self-seeking are always operative in even the most well-intentioned motives—we come to the biblical scriptures with watchful eyes and alert hearts.

Moreover, because we believe that in relationship with God each of us is ultimately responsible for our portion of that partnership, we come to these texts with both curiosity and care. We are curious to know more of our partner, God, as revealed in the relationships others have shared with God. Is this not true of our human relationships? While we value our friends and partners for who they are, we are keenly aware of how those dimensions of our friends and partners are perceived and shared by others. We are rightly pleased and proud when someone we love is lauded and appreciated by coworkers, other friends, and family. And we are duly cautious or reserved when we learn that someone close to us has been dishonest or abusive in other settings. We do not, cannot, inhabit the life of another, no matter how deep our intimacy. We are dependent upon a wide constellation of relationships and their networks to "flesh out" the fullness of another.

Ultimately, however, we rely upon our own best judgment in relationship. We learn, if we are fortunate, how to discern the truth among many, even competing impressions or accounts. We learn that even those we love and trust deeply are no less flawed than us. We hear things about our loved ones that contradict what we know of them. We hear them praised for qualities we've never seen, and we hear them damned, as well. In a complex sorting of information, sometimes processed faster and with greater nuance than possible in any computer, we come to our own judgment. This process of discernment has taught us that if we rely solely upon every piece of information literally, and independent of the other, we are literally torn, incapable of genuine commitment. We accept the muddle, perhaps even welcome it, as defense against intimacy. We leave the jury out, intentionally, lest we be pressed to make a commitment.

Even if we make peace with the contradiction and simply embrace it all uncritically, dismissing contradictions as unimportant, we are still not making a genuine commitment, for we have not committed ourselves to the other person; we have only committed ourselves to a set of opinions, a secondhand relationship at best. At the worst extreme, we become like the abused spouse whose partner appears above reproach in public, but who, in private, is physically violent. We rationalize; we choose to accept only the good report of our partner. We come to believe that we actually deserve the blows, that we should cover them with long sleeves, make-up, and dark glasses to hide our shame and to protect the partner's name. This is not a genuinely loving relationship, nor is it a holy (whole) commitment consonant with what we believe God desires of us, what God desires to give us. God and we deserve better.

We understand the meaning of the Bible, we come to this discernment, by the help of the Holy Spirit, that "third person" proceeding from the heart of relationship as we see it in the bond of God and the Christ. This Spirit guides the church in the true interpretation of the scriptures, helps each of us not only make meaning of our own experiences through the record of previous generations' experience, but gives us a rich, living context—a community—within which our own experience is broadened and deepened.

The power of community learning was impressed upon me by my doctoral studies. The program in which I participated was based upon more than intellectual engagement with books. Our class was limited to eleven, each of us ordained ministers with at least five years of experience in active ministry. Ten of us were from different denominations, and each of us brought to the table the uniqueness of our particular congregations, some parishes, others institutions like campus or hospital chaplaincies. The primary "text" we studied was our own experience. Each of us wrote the story of a particularly challenging, and memorable, experience encountered in ministry, followed by a reflection on that experience parsing and examining its several parts. What elements of this experience, we asked, revealed psychological, sociological, even contextual influences at work in each of the persons in the story, in the communities touched by these stories and experiences? This thoughtful examination sometimes revealed insights into one's own character, or how one had been influenced by some aspect of the other person's behavior or demeanor. It helped me understand how my fears and weaknesses, my biases and ignorance, my denominational traditions, my expectations and assumptions, my ego, my instincts and selfishness—which is to say, my sin—affected the directions and outcomes of the experience. Finally, reflection turned to theology, to the "connections" between this particular story and the larger story, even particular stories within the larger story recorded in biblical scripture. All this was undertaken individually, by each of us, in four different cases or stories prepared each year of the two years we met.

When the eleven of us gathered for the several weeks of our summer time together, we each brought our four stories. Daily we placed two stories before us, one in the morning, one in the afternoon. In sessions of nearly four hours each, we studied the stories and analyses carefully and critically. We agreed that in assessing how each of us had ministered in each case, there was no "right way" or "wrong way." Rather, each person's way had to be examined within the context of his or her understanding of scripture, tradition, and reason and responded to accordingly. Our learnings were rich and varied.

By the end of the second summer, we had studied eighty-eight cases from ten denominations and eleven ministries, not a single one of them in the abstract, but each deeply rooted in human experience and attached to a living person whom we genuinely called friend. Each one of us came away with an enriched understanding of how different communities of Christians interpret scripture and shape their life together in congregations and larger, more complex bodies. And each of us received the gift of perspective beyond the bounds of our own experience.

While this experience was an intentional educational undertaking and represents a highly structured method for learning, it is illustrative of how, in much less formal ways, communities of Christians—some as small as two persons—can and have functioned for centuries as dynamic centers of relationship. Essential to the Christian faith is the simple premise that one cannot be a Christian in isolation. Christianity is intentionally and intensively relational. "Where two or three are gathered in my name," said Jesus, "I am there among them" (Matthew 18:20). Where they are gathered, there is the church.

13

Wonderful
and Sacred Mystery

CHURCH. Though burdened with connotations of institution, few words are as richly descriptive of the phenomenon that sprang from shared experience of the Christ. The Greek root of our English word *church* is *kyrios*, probably one of the most familiar Greek words to practicing Christians, meaning "lord, master." But the word becomes even richer when we press deeper. *Kyrios* is itself derived from the Greek word *kyros*, meaning "power," which my dictionary says is related to the Latin word *cavus*, meaning "hollow," and from which we receive the word *cave*. The richness deepens. Despite the obvious leap that connects our assumptions about early Christian gatherings to holes in the ground, like the catacombs, *cavus* finds its affinity to *kyros*, "power," through another Greek word profoundly associated with power of a specific kind, *kyein*, meaning "to be pregnant."

This brief exploratory word study suggests that the church is not a repository or guarantor of lordly power of the kind we associate with political potency, but the generative womb within which life gestates and matures, awaiting ultimate "birth" into the fullness of life in and with God. It appreciates the church as a creation of relationship. Wherever two or three are gathered in Christ's name, he being in the midst of them, there is this pregnant potentiality we call church, this community embodying, incarnating relationship in the Christ, the Christian covenant.

The Bible describes this gestating potentiality as a body of which Jesus Christ is the head and of which all baptized persons are members. The church in Christian scripture is also called the People of God, the New Israel, a holy nation, a royal priesthood, and the pillar and ground of truth—each of which carries meaning derived from historical context or reaching toward anticipated potency. The church is described in the creeds as one, holy, catholic, and apostolic.

The church is described as one because it is one body, under one head, Jesus Christ. This is not say that this "body" is an organic whole. Most days this body looks like a battlefield casualty, rent asunder, bleeding profusely from every portion and its lordly face barely discernible beneath the tangled mass of hair, flesh, and blood. Yet this still is the body of Jesus Christ, familiar to all who know the tragedy of human self-seeking manifest in institutional power, its consequences evidenced in Jesus upon the cross. It is no less identifiable in this guise, but is perhaps most accessible and approachable for its helplessness.

I have also come to appreciate that the church is well served—and redeemed—by its organic fragmentation. True, the divided church is at one level a scandal, a genuine *skandalon*, which is the Greek word for "stumbling block." But so, maintains Paul and the community of his apostolic succession, is Jesus. Yes, it's an embarrassment. But it's also a threshold, a literal stone that we must stand upon and cross over, or else trip and fall over, or worse, set up as a barrier and stopping place we refuse to surmount. But we cannot ignore it.

I accept the brokenness of the church as the Christian remnant of Babel's tower (Genesis 11). Even Pentecost, the acknowledged "birthday" of the church recounted in Acts, does not grant the church organic unity. Those gathered did not receive a common language; each retained their native tongue. Diversity, the "otherness" essential to relationship, is not obliterated but is in fact upheld. The unity granted is purely spiritual, attainable only in living relationship based upon mutuality, respect, and prodigal self-giving. Any notion that the church can, should, or will achieve organic unity seems to me as emblematic of sin's aspirations as that ill-fated tower in Genesis that sought to reach the divine throne. Any unity, no matter how "holy" in design, is still subject to human sin, can never escape the corruption of our inherent intention toward our own power, our desire to remake the world in our own image, to be (as Genesis astutely observes) "as gods." All our impulses to unity are subject to and tainted by this weakness within us that expects or demands uniformity.

If and when the church can ever be said to be "holy" (whole) it is because the Holy Spirit dwells in it, consecrates its members, guides them to do God's work, and is evidenced in its life, its conduct, its work. That holiness, wholeness, is never assumed, much less presumed. It is always a dependent; it is always evidenced in tangible, incarnate reality—like the fruit hanging on the tree (Luke 6:44).

The church is only truly catholic when it proclaims the whole faith—the full benefit and the full responsibility of relationship with God—to all people, to the end of time. The church is genuinely apostolic when it continues in the teaching and fellowship of the apostles and carries out Christ's mission to all people, not simply in word but also and especially in deed, bearing in the body of each member and in the body of the whole collectively the joy and the burden of prodigal self-giving.

The mission of the church, its *raison d'être*, the only reason for its life and existence, is to restore all people to unity with God and each other as we know that unity in Christ. As such, the church is always and everywhere a means to an end and not an end in itself, a point and perspective frequently lost and only painfully recovered. It is said that the weavers who produce the stunningly intricate rugs we associate with the Middle East, with ancient Persia and environs, intentionally weave a flaw into every carpet as reminder of human imperfection. The flaw inextricably woven into the warp and woof of the church's life is that self-seeking manifest in institutional confusion between means and end. If sin infects every individual human member of the church, it is no less present in the whole, magnified and multiplied when gathered.

If the church's mission is the restoration of relationship between every person and the God who seeks relationship with each of us, this is a mission unattainable by force. Love will not be, cannot be compelled. I have clearly stated above, and here repeat, that the church's mission is to restore all people, each person, to unity with God and with each other *as we know that unity in Christ*. This is a far different thing than making all people "Christian."

This is definitely a contrarian position within Christianity, yet it seems the only position consistent with the "way" taught by Jesus who, despite the limited claims of scripture—themselves compromised by their human agency—never claimed supremacy for himself. His own mission was the same restoration of unity between God and all people, each person, a mission he inherited from his own Judaism and from which he determined not to swerve. It is especially perilous for the church, as institution or denomination, to make any claim of exclusivity, even in the name of Jesus, for such is to place a condition upon the prodigal, unconditional love God offers all. If we learn anything at all from the considerable wisdom of scripture it is *never* to presume to know God's mind, or to place any limit upon God's ways. It has been joked that if you want to hear God laugh, tell God your plans; if you want to invite God's chastening discipline, try passing off your own plans as God's. We are continually reminded, and forcibly taught in the Resurrection, that God's ways are certainly quite different from our ways and not even our most potent and drastic measures can avail against the God who wills to love.

The church then pursues its mission in prayer and worship, proclaiming the gospel—the good news of God's abundant and prodigal love—in reading, studying, reflecting upon, and sharing with others the mighty works of God in the lives of our ancestors and in our own lives, and in the promotion of justice, peace, and love.

This mission is advanced and fulfilled through the ministry of all members of the church. For reason of institutional order these members are divided into several categories of equal status: lay persons, bishops, priests, and deacons. Regardless the category of one's work, the mission of each is the same.

Every Christian is a representation of Christ and his church, just as every member of my family is a representation of all of us who share the same name in the intimacy of a common household, even though that household is scattered farther and farther abroad as we mature and expand the very meaning of family. Each Christian is in himself or herself a full representation of the entire family bearing this common name "Christian," a name bestowed early in our life as a post-Pentecost community, granted by the citizens of Antioch after a prolonged relationship with Barnabas and Paul (Acts 11:26). Thus in all times and places, each of us who claims that name and its inheritance bear witness to the love of God manifest in the Christ wherever we may be; and, according to the gifts given us, we carry on Christ's work of reconciliation in the world.

This work of mission requires constant discernment. Every moment, every encounter, every task offers opportunity to advance our own ends, or to more clearly manifest God's will for us and for the world. Many of us understand the role and discipline of mission; we use it without even thinking about it. For example, the parent who sets out to prepare dinner for the family has many details to consider and tasks to complete. Dinner is the mission, and one's full attention, energy, and ability are given to this mission. Any interruption can deflect that attention and spoil the dinner, wasting precious food and money, and damaging the fabric of the family's relationship gathered at table. Businesses define their missions; if the work of the business is to manufacture stainless steel screws to the highest tolerances for use in strategic applications, like airplanes and automobiles, where the safety of hundreds or thousands of people may rest on the reliability of one small component, then this company must constantly ask of every competing diversion, How does this serve our mission?

Such powers of concentration are constantly at work in each Christian as each moment's demands and diversions prompt the question, How does this serve God's mission of love for the world? This is not always an easy question to answer, in part, because serving others challenges our natural inclination to serve ourselves. And, in part, because serving another requires relationship with the other, being attentive to the other's gifts and needs.

The word *lay* is derived from the Greek *laos* and means, simply, "people." Thus the name applies to all the people of God in the church. The Christian laity is the first and largest order of ministry in the church and, as such, it has the most challenging ministry. It is the most challenging because it is the least bounded or defined, because it is generalized, not specialized. It is a ministry that can and does take every form. In order to bear the burden of this ministry, Christian people take their place in the life, worship, and governance of the church which, because it shares the mission of every Christian, offers a community of support, education, and nurture for the service demanded of ministry.

Even a community of service sharing a common mission and faith cannot long survive without order. As communities grow in number and diversity, some order is necessary and usually arises in response to need. The first and foundational order of the church is the laos, the people of God, whose order is conferred in baptism, about which more will be said later. But it's important to note this common "ordination" at the center of the church's life and order lest the impression be left (or perpetuated) that orders in the church pertain only to certain of its members. Every Christian is ordained, acknowledged as a member of the community and authorized, indeed expected, to carry out its mission.

The order and office of bishop arose of the need for oversight, for that is all that the name means; *bishop* in Greek is *episcopos* and means, literally, "overseer." In any group of talented but diverse and differently abled persons, someone is needed to direct traffic, to see that strengths are mated to weaknesses and all apportioned and appointed in concert to serve the same end, or chaos ensues. The ministry of a bishop is essentially the same as that of every Christian: to represent Christ and his church, but with particular responsibilities. The bishop is elected or selected (depending on denominational order) because this person is perceived, "discerned," by the community to be particularly gifted with the abilities, or "graces," to fulfill the office. Once so selected, the community "ordains" the bishop—the formal act of conferring orders through the laying on of hands by no fewer than three bishops, a sign of assurance that a bishop's ministry and the community "ordering" his or her episcopal ministry is larger than the local diocese. The bishop is thus authorized by the whole communion and the local diocese to oversee its life and order.

The bishop serves as apostle, *apostolos*, meaning "sender" or, to use the more common term, *dispatcher*. In this role, the bishop dispatches the varied gifts of the community to serve the mission of the whole. As chief priest, the bishop is deemed "first among equals" in a community of service whose members are without rank.

As chief *pastor*, a Latin word meaning simply "to feed," the bishop is also first among equals in a community that shares the task of feeding the world and itself—provisioning the world and itself with all the resources needed to carry out the mission of the church within the limited jurisdiction called a diocese. This bounded jurisdiction was created to respond to the reality that there are limits to human oversight; when the community carrying out a mission grows too large and complex, it is neither reasonable nor possible to expect it to function effectively, much less efficiently. The bishop's responsibility to guard the faith, unity, and discipline of the whole church is described as a function of pastoring and, understood within this context of feeding, may be aptly described as keeping everyone at the table. Having grown up as one of five children who shared a table daily with our parents, I can attest that this is no simple task.

The remaining work of the bishop is, again, that of all the people of God: to proclaim the Word of God; to act in Christ's name for the reconciliation of the world and the building up of the church. But one more authority is reserved to the bishop, who is entrusted to ordain others to continue Christ's ministry.

While there is much uncertainty about the role and rite of Confirmation among modern Anglicans, this ministry reserved to the bishop could be seen as a form of ordination. Confirmation (*BCP*, p. 413) and its associated ritual acts of Reception and Reaffirmation of Baptismal Vows are rites by which a baptized person may affirm his or her commitment to life in the church. They are rites associated with adulthood and the mature acceptance of responsibility for one's life in community. As such, they represent a specific and personal commitment to lay ministry, and, while not formally included in the "ordering" of ministries, certainly seem to belong to that category.

But the more prominent episcopal authority is the ordering of priests and deacons. These ministries, consistent with those of the laity and the bishops, represent Christ and his church. The priest, like the bishop, is particularly called and charged to be pastor (feeder) to the people, to share the bishop's overseeing of the church, proclamation of the gospel, administration of the sacraments, blessing and declaring pardon in the name of God. While the ministries of bishop and priest are nearly identical, they differ in scope. The priest, like the bishop and every lay member of the church, is expected to extend ministry to all people. But just as the bishop is given jurisdiction of a diocese, so the priest is "ordered" to the jurisdiction of a congregation—a smaller division of a diocese. The ministry of the priest is thus a delegation of the bishop's ministry and authority.

The English word *priest* and its older, Latin and Greek root, *presbyter*, mean "elder." In some ways both are inferior to the word *parson*, an old English corruption of the word "person." The parson is the person in whom a community or congregation of Christians is embodied; the parson is the vicarious representative of both the bishop and the "parish," the people of a particular congregation. (By way of digression, the term *vicar*, encountered in literature and still retained in some Episcopal dioceses, denotes the pastor of a mission or aided congregation. Canonically, parish status denotes a congregation's financial and governing independence; mission or aided congregations tend to be financially dependent upon, and their local governance more directly accountable to, the diocese. Moreover, the diocese may hold deed to a mission congregation's property. Thus, the bishop is technically the chief pastor of any such congregation and the local pastor is literally the bishop's vicar—the vicarious representative of the bishop in that place.)

The identification of a parish as one congregation gathered in a church building and bearing a particular denominational identity is certainly a fairly recent innovation in Christian life and order. Successive fractures of Christianity into discrete communities or coalitions united by defined creed or doctrine and canonical authority, and the commingling of non-Christian religious communities within a single culture, present a challenge to structural definitions that seem to have ignored such pluralism. The word *parish* is an interesting merging of Greek words that in combination literally mean "a household of strangers" and was originally used in the church as a geographical division, a division within a "diocese"—whose root is also richly connected to "housekeeping"—the geographically bounded area of a bishop's authority and oversight.

Thus, while it is possible to see within such embracing words a certain presumptive blindness to religious difference or an imperial arrogance, one might also see within these words an inclusive embrace. A parson's responsibility extends to everyone within the bounds of the geographical parish—not just to the small subset of that community that voluntarily associates with a specific congregation. For indeed, from an evangelical perspective, if the mission of the church is to reunite all persons, each person, with God, then this mission extends well beyond the particularity of a single congregation.

Because this broader definition of parish embraces far more than any one person can be expected to bear, it is all the more important that we understand the parish not as a building or even a household into which an entire community is gathered, but as the locus from which ministry is literally carried out to the larger community. The mission of the church is not to make all human beings members of the church, but rather, as the church, to live in all times and all places as if the entire community *is* the household of God. It is mission oriented outward, like the generously self-giving God in whose name we are sent.

If the mission of the church is to leaven the world as yeast leavens bread (Matthew 13:33; 1 Corinthians 5:6; Galatians 5:9) and to season the whole earth as salt seasons the dish (Matthew 5:13; Mark 9:50; Luke 14:34), then the work of the local congregation is to maintain the kind of potency necessary to the task. And the work of the pastor is to provision, to feed the congregation.

The images of servanthood pervade the ancient Christian understanding of ministry but are often lost in contemporary structures and practices. Indeed, the demands of this servanthood were so pressing upon the earliest bishops and priests that a separate order was called to assist in the essential outreach beyond the congregation.

The *deacon* (literally Greek for "servant"), like laity, bishop, and priest, represents Christ and his church, but particularly as a servant of those in need. In the ritual life of the local congregation, the deacon is also authorized to assist bishops and priests in the proclamation of the gospel and the administration of the sacraments. Reserving the liturgical reading of the gospel to the deacon is a ritual anachronism; in times and cultures where literacy may have been limited to clergy, it certainly made sense to place this responsibility upon those best able to read the gospel clearly and intelligently. But in a literate society and within congregations whose lay readers competently proclaim the other scriptural readings in the liturgy, there is little necessity to preserve this distinction.

Moreover, the role of the deacon beyond the walls of the church might be greatly expanded, and the mission of the church furthered, by encouraging their creative deployment in the organization and administration of the congregation's outreach not only in the obvious ministries of charity and compassion, but in all instances where lay members of the church need assistance in their ministries. Gifted deacons can and often do serve specialized arenas of ministry like hospitals and prisons, both providing their own pastoral services and coordinating the deployment of lay ministers in these settings. Deacons may be deployed to campus ministry, youth and camp ministry, and workplace ministries which often falter or fail for lack of coordination and administration, which are also expressions of servanthood to those in need, especially when we expand the definition of "need" to include the lack of spiritual resources and the physical presence of incarnational organization.

All the orders of ministry—lay, episcopal, presbyteral, and diaconal—are expressions of servanthood; the word *minister* means "servant." The church and all its ministries, it has been said, exist only for the sake of the world beyond the walls of the churches. It is that world we are to serve and we are each called to that service in our relationship with God. All ministries exist to serve the mission of the church, the mission of the Christ to all humans which is the reunion of each person to relationship with God. For the love of God, we bear this responsibility. Which is to say that we've been given the ability to respond to God's love for us; our response to God's prodigal self-giving is to become prodigally self-giving.

But we are not God. We are limited creatures, our lives bounded by mortality. This limitation we share with the Christ, who calls us to follow, who calls us to give our lives, live our lives prodigally, without fear of mortality. This life we share with the Christ, who calls us to follow in trust, with confidence that even mortality itself is powerless to overcome us. Still, we are creatures of faith, living our lives in trust; thus to follow the Christ we come together week by week for corporate worship. We work, pray, and give for the mission of God.

14

Talking the Talk, Walking the Walk

CONVERSATION IS A RICH WORD derived from a Latin verb meaning "to live, keep company with." An essential component of relationship, conversation takes many forms. For the person in relationship with God, *prayer* is a conversational encounter with God expressed in thought and/or deeds, with or without words. Christians enjoy a lively relationship with God, as God is met in and through Jesus the Christ, and as both are experienced in the influence of the Holy Spirit.

Jesus encouraged conversation with God, practicing and providing the example of prayer in a specific form now known as the Lord's Prayer (*BCP*, p. 364). The principal kinds of prayer are defined by the church as adoration, praise, thanksgiving, penitence, oblation, intercession, and petition. These somewhat arcane technical divisions are about as practical, and boring, as the grammar of any language. Most of us learned the difference between affirmative, interrogative, and exclamatory sentences, but we hardly bring these distinctions to mind when engaged in stimulating conversation with a loved one.

Still, they can be helpful tools when navigating the complexities of language in relationship. The practiced writer, whether putting pen to paper or fingers to a keyboard, knows that one needs a balance of all types of sentence to make a good, interesting paragraph or page. Or, to mix metaphors, the different types of prayer, like the different foods, are needed in balance for good nutrition. Too many questions or exclamations, like too many fats or carbohydrates, can be ruinous. So let's examine the mix.

Adoration is a posture of openness to God that seeks only to enjoy God's presence. Easier said than done, this seemingly simple and somewhat passive form of prayer is the product of long relationship and deep trust. What commonly passes for adoration is a vacuous moonfaced piety, the religious version of a thoroughly smitten infatuation. God is not an insatiable egotist who demands to be doted upon; God seeks a mature partnership, the kind of ease shared between partners of long history. Rightly practiced, adoration is a dangerous form of prayer, for to enter a conversation openly, receptive to hear the other, to receive the other's presence fully, is to make oneself vulnerable to change. Adoration requires no words, but delights in the sheer and dangerous intimacy of the other's closeness. It is the practice of being alone together, an intimacy with which most of us are decidedly uncomfortable.

Similarly, *praise* is not an effusive outpouring of superlatives combined with a good measure of toady obeisance, but is instead an expression of appreciation for all that we share in and with God. One can accord right value to God without resorting to vain flattery. Jesus is said to have met a man who greeted Jesus as "Good Teacher," despite any evidence that the two had any prior relationship (Mark 10:17ff.; Luke 18:18ff.). The man is described as rich, and presumably important, yet Jesus is neither. Jesus senses an idle flattery at work and gently sets the greeting aside, suggesting that only God deserves the kind of praise he's just received. The greeting is inflated, out of proportion to the reality of their relationship; it's a secondhand compliment; the greeter is maneuvering—seeking a favor, and attempting to justify asking this favor of one so obviously beneath him by inflating Jesus' stature with his praise.

Jesus responds that true praise is more than words. It is evidenced in action. In this case, the rich man is counseled to practice the radical prodigality of God—give all the riches away, says Jesus. Paradoxically, equality or parity in partnership with God is not achieved by ratcheting up the praise, but by emptying oneself until one is reduced to the stature of God. Only then does one approach righteousness, blessedness, wholeness. In the collection of sayings on blessedness attributed to Jesus known as "The Beatitudes" (Matthew 5), the first reads "Blessed are the poor in spirit, for theirs in the kingdom of God." I prefer the rendering of the New English Bible, "How blest [happy] are those who know their need of God." From that need, that emptiness, we arrive at the next form of prayer, *thanksgiving*.

Thanksgiving acknowledges God as the source of all the blessings of this life, the source and force of redemption—the one who first seeks reconciliation and reunion with us, and perseveres against all odds to draw us closer in love. This is another form of prayer too frequently obscured, and avoided, by words. Yes, I may and should tell my partner and my friends how very thankful I am for their love, but the sincerest form of gratitude for their love is simply to receive it.

Despite our many cries to the contrary, most of us are wary of being loved. We do not deem ourselves worthy, or we judge ourselves too busy or too good to be bothered with the commitment, or all of the above. Love just does not come easily to us. We can't be bothered or beholden; we're not worth the bother. We have too much need of love, or too little. Whatever the reason, we defend ourselves against the intrusion of love. And we offer words of thanks with little or no sincerity to the God who is most eloquently and adequately thanked in our reception of the gift.

When we are brave and bold enough to acknowledge our resistance, we come to *penitence*; we confess our resistance and seek restitution where possible, and the changing of our ways. Penitence, too, is largely a nonverbal posture. To repent is simply to turn around. If sin is resistance to God's love, a willful turning away from God, an assumption of our own self-sufficiency, then penitence is a literal turning around. It is to cease flight, to reverse one's orientation. Stopped, standing still, facing the God from whom we have fled, we are in the posture for *oblation.*

Oblation means "offering," and a prayer of oblation is an offering of oneself, one's life and labors, for God's mission. This is a very active, tangible form of prayer, prayer in deed. Jesus told of the difference between word and deed in the story of a father and two sons. The father asked the first son one day to work the vineyard. The son refused, but later went and did as asked. The father went to the second son with the same request. The second son promised to do the work, but never got around to it (Matthew 21:28ff.). Which son, asked Jesus, actually *did* the father's will?

The last two forms of prayer are often verbal. *Intercession* articulates the needs of others; *petition* expresses our own needs. Why say any prayer aloud? Surely God has no need to hear us; to God, as we say in the Collect for Purity (*BCP*, p. 355), "all hearts are open, all desires known, and from [God] no secrets are hid."

Each week I stand in community and offer prayers by name for those I know who live with HIV/AIDS, other progressive diseases or any illness, those who are in danger or imprisoned, and those who suffer for any reason. I do not say their names for God's sake, but for my own and for my community, my immediately family in God who help me bear the weight of these people and their concerns. I repeat their names aloud as reminder to myself of each one's presence in my life and the precious cords that connect us in love. I remember them and *re-member* them—bring them into consciousness and into the midst of our assembly—in the powerful repetition of name, the name granted them at birth and affirmed before God. Realistically, practically, I know that what I can do for each of these persons is severely limited. It is not within my power to cure them, to remove their illnesses, to reverse their circumstances, to rehabilitate the brokenness of their lives and free them from their prisons. But I can re-member them.

The least I can do, and sometimes the most, is to offer them a place in my day, in my heart, in the midst of this family gathered at table. So potent is this form of prayer for those named that they some-times tell me they feel the connection, know themselves to be loved even from afar. So dynamic is this form of prayer that after months, even years, of praying for one who is sick, those named become in-visible but tangible members of the community. I have more than once quietly moved a name from the intercessions for the sick to the intercessions for those who have died only to see the eyes of some in the congregation fill with tears, and to be greeted by them at the ex-change of the peace or at the door with words of condolence for me, sharing their own grief that someone they have known for so long, though never met, has gone from them and this life.

Petitions for ourselves may seem a vanity and, sadly, they often are. But if we believe that God has endowed us with freedom, and that God so respects us that God would not breech that liberty, then we need somehow to grant God permission to meddle in our affairs. Petition is the means by which we invite God's involvement in the specifics of our lives. In even the closest, most intimate relationships, we must still articulate our needs, must ask for help. Remembering to ask God for help, offering prayers of petition for our own needs, can lead us to humility and remind us to ask those whom God has given us to assist us in our need.

Despite my love for words and my affection for an Anglican tra-dition richly steeped in the pages of a prayer book, I am convinced that in prayer, less is truly more. In the ongoing conversation with God, I cannot listen if I am busy framing my argument or searching about for my response. In daily intimacy with God, I need not natter on about everything, for endless babbling only holds the other at arm's length. Side by side, day by day, I find the richest relationship and conversation in that quiet being together that grows deeper as the years lengthen. But I am also aware of my need to venture beyond the confines of this intimacy, for I am still very much in this world and while God's relationship with me—and mine with God—is personal, it is not exclusive.

This is why most spiritualities and pieties that rely on the imagery of romantic love suffer the fate of our metaphorical three-legged dog. They cannot stay the course, in part, because the intensity of sexual desire and the exclusivity of the intimate sexual commitment are neither reliable nor universal. Sexual desire is only a component of love, subject to circumstance and variable intensity. Moreover, exclusive intimate sexual partnership, while known to many, is neither given to nor chosen by all.

Nor is "family" language or imagery any more helpful or appropriate. Certainly not if, by family, we mean a narrowly described tribe. Jesus challenges and unsettles our notions of family. In a stunning gospel account, "his mother and his brothers came; and standing outside, they sent to him and called him. A crowd was gathered around him; and they said to him, 'Your mother and your brothers and sisters are outside, asking for you.' And he replied, 'Who are my mother and my brothers?' And looking at those who sat around him, he said, 'Here are my mother and my brothers!'" (Mark 3:31ff.).

Jesus' radical redefinition of family, and the Christian mission to bring all into union with God, are extroverted challenges to all our introverted tendencies. Much as I'd love to cocoon in cozy comfort with my God, or bask in the ease of assured kinship, sooner or later I must take my place in the world. This requires discipline, and practice. That practice is corporate worship, wherein individual Christian believers unite to acknowledge the wholeness they share in God, to hear God's Word in the stories of generations of believers, and to offer prayer.

I confess that I do not always find worship satisfying or entertaining. Indeed, if worship is to be genuinely edifying—which means "to instruct or improve spiritually"—it should challenge me. Like good teaching, good worship will not simply lecture to me, but will encourage, even demand, that I invest myself. Thus, the most important aspect of corporate worship is simply being there.

I realized this while a student in seminary chafing under the obligation of daily chapel. Day after day I went dutifully, often wondering why I wasn't somewhere else, doing something else. But as my relationships with and awareness of others grew, I became aware of the absences. When prayers were offered for those in hospital, or the ones called home suddenly for an emergency, or any of the many reasons for absence, I was mindful of their unfilled place. When friends were not present, I missed them. Gradually I realized that while I may have little to give, I could take my place at the table. I could be there and, in being there, give and receive, participate in the discipline of a shared life, which is the first step in the fulfillment of the mission to restore all to unity in God.

But this practice has its drills. As a music student I learned to play scales on the piano, and was challenged to practice *études*, little pieces of music incorporating basic techniques and written to test those skills. Ideally, one's practice and mastery of these basics were transferable. When the same techniques were encountered in a long composition, the odd bits practiced discretely came together in a unified whole.

Christian worship and its rituals and sacraments have many dimensions, including their role as the *études* of a faithful life. When the church celebrates—performs—a sacrament, mystical or miraculous possibilities are always present. But then, that could be said of every occasion in life. What may not be so apparent is the basic practicality of *sacrament*, a word that at base means "obligation," a word one normally associates with discipline and practice.

The church defines sacraments as outward and visible signs of inward and spiritual grace, given by the Christ as sure and certain means by which we receive that grace. Grace is another of those words in the Christian vocabulary that is freely used and seldom defined, a word whose meaning is assumed to be transparent but even among Christians is variously understood. For many, grace is equated with good fortune, frequently material—financial security, health, and general well-being.

Grace is closely akin to the word *mercy*, the latter derived from an ancient word for "market." Thus the instinct that equates grace and mercy with trade and commodity is deeply rooted in our language and intellect. Both words have so long been used and abused by the church that one must plow through the dictionaries' several definitions specific to religion to recover basic meanings of each useful in framing an understanding of God.

I have found it helpful to consider grace not as something that is given to us or that happens to *us* but rather to conceive grace as the eternal posture of *God*, the perpetual attitude of God. Deeply embedded in the word *grace* is its ancient antecedent: *gratia*, the Latin word for "thanks," root of "gratitude." Returning to the story of creation in Genesis, we recall a God whose creativity evoked the deep pleasure of joy, issuing in the frequent exclamation "It is good!" The creator's appreciation, gratitude for the beauty, joy—even fun—of creativity, is captured in that simple outburst repeated with the appearance of each new creature.

Grace describes the perpetual joy and welcome of God, the posture of the prodigal God always open to receive and appreciate. Grace as we encounter it in human hospitality is much the same. The tale is told of an untutored commoner invited to dine at a monarch's table. After several delectable courses had been served and enjoyed, the servers appeared with the finger bowls. A dainty cup was placed before each diner, each vessel filled with a clear steaming liquid in which floated a perfect slice of lemon.

The hapless guest lifted the cup to his lips and sipped. His companions at table sat aghast and some, amused by his ignorance, quietly smiled at one another. All eyes turned toward the monarch who, without hesitation, lifted her cup and sipped. That's grace. Divine grace. And a parable of the Incarnation.

The legendary monarch would not allow any protocol to marginalize or exclude the guest; in one gracious act, the constricting boundaries of etiquette were shattered to make room, to allow the full inclusion and participation of the one. The story is an echo of Jesus' parable of one lost sheep, told in Luke, chapter fifteen. It moves us to perceive grace as the prodigal God's delight in us, affection and appreciation unearned and undeserved—and thus completely unrelated to merit or market value. Because grace is a quality of *God*, the space within which God meets us, makes room for us, it is beyond our manipulative commodification. We can't buy it with money or deeds. We'll never merit it, aren't entitled to it, for it is always gift, the gift of the extravagant, abundant, giving God. As such, God's grace offers us abundant room, unbounded space unconditionally open to us without regard for our sins—for that is what true *forgiveness* means: a capacity within which no claim for requital, no resentment or recompense is admitted. Only love is allowed there. And us.

To stand in such a place, to be so embraced, enlightens our minds, stirs our hearts, and strengthens our wills. Yet we live, move, and have our being in another space, one bounded by time and our mortality. How do we stand, much less live, in both simultaneously? In the practice of sacrament. A sacrament is not magic, not even a rite. *Sacrament* means "to make holy, to set apart." The basic and essential element of the Christian sacraments is *the space*. What is first and fundamentally set apart in a sacrament is the space itself. That may, of course, be a church. But it need not be. A sacrament is always and everywhere a space wherein we practice living in that abundant, unbounded span unconditionally open to us without regard for our sins. The two sacramental spaces foundational to the Christian life are Baptism and Eucharist.

15

To Live in Christ, Instead of Death

S ACRAMENTS ARE A CREATION of the church, a product of life in community. This is an assertion not shared by all Christians, but one I believe essential to a proper humility. Sacramental rites are human inventions within a larger human invention, the institutional church. As such, they are doubly suspect, twice as susceptible to the tendency of all things human to seek self-serving power. Sacraments have been and continue to be abused, for they are human instrumentalities entrusted to human agents. Like all creation, the church and its sacraments are imbued with freedom and may thus be used to good, gracious, and godly purposes or to selfish, destructive, and demonic ends.

Moreover, as a creation of the church, sacraments are only media: they are always a means and never ends in themselves, else they would violate the biblical injunctions forbidding idolatry. We are encouraged to present ourselves to God and to seek and see God in and through the sacraments. They offer passage and a place to meet and be met.

Sacraments represent the response of the faithful to the challenge and the joy of life in God. They are spaces created and deemed holy by the church, not simply because we say so; they are holy because and only when we offer those spaces wholly to God. They are literally extraordinary spaces dedicated—given to—the practice of living God's abundant, self-giving, unconditional, prodigal love. They are our "practice rooms," within which we practice the abundant life God holds out to us so that we might more effectively live that abundant, prodigal life everywhere, all the time.

Baptism is the sacrament, the holy space, within which we affirm and accede to God's affirmation of us as God's own children. Our acceptance of God's affirmation makes us members of Christ's body, the church. In our affirmation and acceptance of God we participate in the vocation of Jesus, whose own radical affirmation and acceptance of relationship with God marks him as the Christ. In our baptismal affirmation we practice solidarity with the Christ—we make our own incarnational commitment literally to place our bodies, ourselves, in the same relationship with God evidenced in Jesus himself. We take our place within that space at the heart of God.

When I visit a place, occupy its space, my presence leaves an impression on that place—and that place leaves its imprint in me. Like all sacraments of the church, the space and rite of baptism is a signet. As the signet pressed into warm wax sealed a documented promise or proclamation, so baptism represents a signet upon one's life. In the occupation of that holy space, and the imposition of the sign of the cross in oil upon the forehead, one becomes a documented citizen of the church and bears thereafter the mark of membership in and with the Christ. Baptism is a ceremony of citizenship, a ritual by which and within which one accepts both the rights *and* the responsibilities of membership.

"To live in Christ, instead of death." That is how the wise lay theologian, the late William Stringfellow, described the uniqueness of the Christian life, the baptized life. The sacrament of baptism, the momentary space within which one's relationship with God and God's relationship with us, is affirmed and ratified, is a space of remarkable, mutual self-giving. Within that space Christians practice, and commit to the perpetual practice of, continual self-giving in relationship with their generous, gracious God. It is a conscious choice and commitment for both God and us, signified in an exchange of names, the significance of which is recalled in the story of Jacob's long night of wrestling with a mysterious stranger at Peniel (Genesis 32:22ff.).

In that story, the surrender of his name was Jacob's last, desperate surrender of self, submission to ultimate vulnerability. The mysterious, unnamed stranger denies Jacob any reciprocity, though the implication of the story makes clear that this mysterious, unnamed stranger is none other than God.

Against that background, Christian baptism represents a powerful exchange of names. At baptism we accept and affirm the name by which we are known in the human family, our Christian or baptismal "first" name. If an infant, the name is given by our parents and sponsors. If of age, it is given by the person being baptized. The name is repeated aloud in the assembly, and as water is poured over us or as we are lowered into it, to our first name is added our family name: the name and family of Father, Son, and Holy Spirit. That's a rather unwieldy surname, but God affirms our place within the eternal space of unbounded love, names us as children and heirs, and gives us the name sealing—signifying—our relationship, our place in the family of God.

The outward and visible sign, the material element, in baptism is water, in which a person is *baptized* (literally, "dipped") in the name of the Trinity: the Father, the Son, and the Holy Spirit. That ritual dipping represents one's union with the Christ in his death and resurrection, entrance into God's family, the church, into the abundant, unbounded space of God's grace and into a new life animated by the Spirit. Though we are creatures of time and mortality, living in this bounded life and world, we affirm and accept our place within that eternal, unbounded life of God. We commit to live within that unbounded life of God even in the midst of this bounded world of time and death. Or as William Stringfellow says it, we commit "to live in Christ, instead of death." That commitment is marked by a series of renunciations and promises.

The first is a renunciation "of Satan and all the spiritual forces of wickedness that rebel against God." Who or what is "Satan"? At least one thing may be asserted of Satan, and that is that whatever Satan may be, Satan is no equal to God. Neither we nor the universe is entangled in a warring contention between God and some equal, opposing force. Even the biblical authors of the Book of the Revelation posited that God does not do combat with Satan; that work is delegated to archangelic creatures (Chapter 12).

Satan may be no more, and is certainly no less, than the collective forces of human resistance to and rebellion against God. Satan, who also goes by the name "the devil"—a word derived from the Greek word for "slander"—represents all that is contrary to truth. Satan isn't just a liar; Satan is LIE personified, the incarnation of untruth. Thus, as legend has it, Satan hates the light, seeks power and control over liberty and grace. And as the myth of the archangel Lucifer's rebellion maintains, Satan is good's potential gone bad. To return to Stringfellow's formula, Satan lives in death, instead of Christ—seeks self and the transient, illusive power of bounded time and space instead of the self-giving, eternal boundlessness of God.

The second renunciation, of "the evil powers of this world which corrupt and destroy the creatures of God," is an extension of the first. It is a repudiation of the destructive, corrosive impulses that are antithetical to creativity, corruption and destruction being the opposite of health and creativity. Note also that the renunciation is of "powers of this world," the world bounded by time and mortality. That is not a renunciation of time and mortality, but of the destructive and corrupt potential inherent in everything therein. If, after all, we are affirming our partnership with God, our role as partners, like that of physicians, is first to do no harm. We acknowledge our potential for mischief and mistake, and our renunciation alerts and awakens us to vigilance.

A third renunciation, of "all sinful desires that draw [us] from the love of God" goes deeper, beyond rebellious act and rebellious potential to rebellious desire. These impulses are the hardest to give up, the most difficult to eradicate, in part because they are often beyond the reach of sheer will power. What we are renouncing is an element of our freedom, for the freedom endowed at creation includes the liberty to deny God, to refuse God's love and relationship. I appreciate especially the specificity of the baptismal rite that repudiates as sinful all desires that entice or compel us from God's love. In this specificity we are called to consider every desire that denies the gift God offers us so generously—all those exertions of will and want that ultimately disappoint us, that fail to fulfill or sustain us because they hold God at arm's length. They are the substitutions we place between us and the God who loves us. To read a powerful, timeless, and sexually charged parable of this human tendency, look again at the biblical book of Hosea. In that story a spouse's rampant marital infidelity and sexual license in the face of a prodigally boundless and steadfast partner's love become a parable of how stubborn, destructive, and heartbreaking our desires can be.

The next affirmation, interestingly, is specific to posture: "Do you turn to Jesus Christ and accept him as your Savior?" Reorientation positions the believer "face to face" with the Christ and with God. The physicality is striking and might be reinforced in the rite itself by a corresponding physical movement. But the initial step toward acceptance, and embrace, is to cease one's active opposition, one's running from, and to turn toward the One offering a place.

The baptismal candidate is then asked, "Do you put your whole trust in his [the Christ's] grace and love?" The bold assertion of total self-giving is too great a thing to be so succinctly distilled. Of course, do any of us realize at the point of making a promise the full import of what we pledge? The pledge of one's *whole* trust is a promise of total commitment which, once given, leaves no trust for investment elsewhere. What does this leave for those earthly commitments, like that unto a partner or spouse? Such a sweeping and inclusive pledge does not diminish or compete with our other commitments, but is consistent with the belief that all love and trust is an expression of God's love and trust, participates in the divine loving and trusting from which everything is created and within which everything is sustained.

Lastly, the candidate is asked, "Do you promise to follow and obey [the Christ] as *your* Lord." I have emphasized the personal possessive pronoun which is used where one might expect to see the definite article *the*. Central to the promise is my personal pledge to enter fully the life of (to follow and obey, or trust) the Christ as *my* Lord. This pledge defines my relationship with the Christ neither as exclusive possession nor as universal assumption. In other words, while I agree to the Christ's role in my life, I can neither claim that as uniquely, solely mine, nor can I assume or presume to impose a similar relationship on others who may not have chosen that relationship freely for themselves.

The word *Lord* demands some additional exploration. Imbued with the political and social accretions of human governance and power, this word has been rejected by some as detrimental to relationship with God. Again, rooting around in the word proves helpful. *Lord* is an Old English elision of words meaning "loaf" (as in bread) and "keeper." This rich association with feeding and overseeing or safeguarding links the word to its oft-used biblical synonym *shepherd*. Thus to accept and embrace the Christ as my Lord need not mean a slavish obedience to an overbearing superiority, but rather, a further expression of my abiding trust in the Christ as the ultimate source of my own sustenance and safety. To follow and obey the Christ wholly is to embrace his own fully trusting relationship with God, whom even Jesus called "shepherd." For God is the only shepherd allowed by scripture, the source of our life and safety. To embrace and accept the Christ as my loaf and keeper (or loaf-keeper) is to pray with my own self the prayer he himself taught me to pray, to the God who both gives and is my daily bread, who delivers me, safeguards me from all evil.

Having made these extravagant promises, the baptismal candidate is momentarily and forcefully reminded of the space of this sacrament, when all those present pledge in unison, and often loudly, to support this person in his or her life in Christ. Quite suddenly, in this swift shift of attention, all are reminded that this space, the church gathered, is a community practicing the radical generosity of God's love. Practicing. Working at it. Together. In this space and in this moment, for sure, but presumably in all the world and in every moment. All have taken the same extravagant promises; all possess the same freedom and inherent potential for success and failure in the maintenance of these vows. And at this point, all get into the act, all are drawn back to the central promises that make them who and what they are: children of God, members of God's household, heirs and inhabitants of God's boundless life and love we call eternity.

After a shared recitation of the creed, that splendidly earthen vessel within which we attempt to name the God who is beyond all naming, the baptismal candidate(s) continue their promises, but now joined by the entire assembly. Together they rehearse the promises that frame their practice.

They pledge to "continue in the apostles' teaching and fellowship, in the breaking of bread, and in the prayers." In sum, they pledge to remain at the table, where the scriptures are read, the stories are told—not just the ancient tales, but the continuing, present-day stories that witness to the great things God continues to do in our lives. They pledge to remain at table, breaking bread and offering prayer.

"Will you persevere in resisting evil, and, whenever you fall into sin, repent and return to the Lord?" they are asked. Having made this pledge by oneself, the baptismal candidate is now joined by an entire community pledged to an equal perseverance, and a frank admission of how weak that resolve can be. The rite does not read, "if you fall into sin," but "whenever you fall into sin," a bold acknowledgment of hard reality. The resolve to commit wholly and to renounce entirely always understands the continual nature of this promise and the perpetual difficulty of mediating human life, a life bounded by death and mortality, with God's boundless, fearless love.

Together, all pledge to "proclaim by word and example the Good News of God in Christ." This proclamation which forms the center of Christian life together is usually the one most neglected. That is not a criticism of the reluctance to evangelize, or the reticence in public that marks an extremely "proper" personal faith. Neither is it to encourage evangelical aggression or a public assertiveness of the type associated with the opposing extreme of enthusiastic faith. Rather, it is to say that the central activity of "table talk" is missing from our lives.

I grew up in a large family of five children with two active parents. In our family and nearly every group I've ever known gathered over and around food, the bounty of the table is matched or even surpassed by an abundance of conversation, the words and stories that feed us in ways that food cannot. These are the words and stories that link our lives to those no longer living, the ancestors remembered at the family gathering, whose antics and wisdoms continue to enliven us. These are also the words and stories that bind us to one another, the visions and the sadnesses shared, the joys and hopes multiplied, the love and affection manifest, incarnate in others. Our words and our thoughtful ways with one another continually proclaim the good news of God in Christ, give continual and palpable evidence of our experience of and trust in the abundant life and love of God.

The proclamation practiced in our gathering prepares us for and sustains us beyond the table. If we are enjoined to any extroversion, it is in our promise to seek and serve Christ in all persons, loving our neighbor as our self. Like the summary of the law upon which the promise is based, this loving is predicated upon love of oneself—upon one's own acceptance of worth and dignity expressed and acknowledged in God's love for us. We are not to hold this love closely to ourselves but, in emulation of the Christ and God, and in fulfillment of our pledge to live in that prodigality, we are to actively seek and serve others as we have been sought and served in and by God in the Christ. Gently, patiently, we are called to persevere in that quietly compelling love that seeks no requital, sets no condition.

Lastly, and most dauntingly, the community joins the baptismal candidate in a final pledge to "strive for justice and peace among all people, and respect the dignity of every human being." Well, we've certainly got our work cut out for us, haven't we? Acknowledging that this is not simply a matter of will or human perseverance, but a superhuman task demanding our best efforts and then some, each promise is buttressed with an invocation of God's help. Not only does the phrase "with God's help" acknowledge dependence upon God for the keeping of these expansive promises, the phrase is also an invitation to God, a welcoming of God's partnership without which God would never intrude.

All of this seems reasonable enough for thoughtful adults. But many Christian churches baptize infants. How are we to make any sense of infant baptism? Certainly not as a preventive of damnation, not if we believe that God has made everything; this affirmation holds that every child conceived and born is already of God, is beloved by God.

The sacramental power of infant baptism is—and perhaps should be intentionally and liturgically—linked to human families, to parents and congregations. This was made apparent to me quite by accident. As a university chaplain I was asked to baptize a new infant. The parents requested that the baptism take place in the campus chapel where they had wed. It was a lovely setting, a stunning example of restored colonial American architecture, but it lacked a baptismal font.

As I pondered the logistical challenge, a solution emerged gradually from a simple accession to practical necessity. I had recently come into possession of a very large and handsome bowl crafted of local clay and fired in a glaze consistent with the locale. That would be our font. As we took our places in chapel, the husband, the wife, and I stood at the end of the aisle just beneath the first and lowest chancel step—exactly where we had stood on their wedding day. I faced the congregation; husband and wife faced each other as they had on the day when, as bride and groom, they had taken their vows. Now we were joined by their child.

After the recitation of the promises, the father took the bowl from a waiting acolyte, faced his wife, and held it. The mother held the child suspended over the bowl (face down, as I've learned that few infant creatures much like being flipped upon their backs), and I recited the baptismal formula as I scooped handfuls of water to drench the baby's head. In that moment I was impressed by the simple truth being visibly confessed in this holy space.

This young father and mother, fresh with the pride of childbirth, had returned to the site of their wedding pledge and the sacred space of sacramental community, there to acknowledge publicly the cooperative agency of God in the creation and life of their child. With humility and dignity they were professing that they, of their own creative energies and initiative, could not claim this child as only their own; they acknowledged and thanked God for the partnership all shared in this wondrous miracle. As they had on their wedding day, they were making promises in the company of others, pledging themselves and the community with them, to rear this child within this truth they perceived and believed. This child would be reared in the context of God's unbounded, unconditional love, by parents and a community committed to living in that trust.

Baptism is then a potent symbolic expression of human humility and divine creativity, of shared partnership in creation and affirmation of God's prevenient love for every child—love that precedes the creative act itself. The prevenient affection of God is an anticipatory love consistent with the extravagant prodigality of this generous God, whose love is extended *before* the making, not withheld against some future judgment.

Thus seen, baptism is not a prophylactic against limbo or any other intermediate status on the way to ultimate damnation. I am aware that this is a radical departure from a significant body of theology. But I am also mindful that that theology is the product of an institutional church whose insistence upon baptism as initiatory rite of membership grants that human institution a power that has frequently led to abuse, spiritual and otherwise. The prayer Jesus taught respectfully petitions that God's will be done on earth as it is in heaven; there is scant warrant that earth be granted the power to exert its will upon heaven.

The grant of power to human agency may attach to certain scriptural injunctions, most notably Matthew 16:19, where Jesus is reputed to have granted to Peter "the keys of the kingdom of heaven," and says to Peter "whatever you bind on earth will be bound in heaven, and whatever you loose on earth will be loosed in heaven." Matthew's gospel also includes an injunction to "Go therefore and make disciples of all nations, baptizing them in the name of the Father and of the Son and of the Holy Spirit."

Both of these passages are now and have long been disputed, the first because of the emphasis that Roman Catholic tradition attaches to this claim as a basis for papal authority, and the latter because it appears to have been a later addition to the original gospel. My own suspicion of them stems from their association with claims related to institutional power and control, claims that contradict an overwhelming evidence for God's prodigal generosity.

My suspicion of the church is by no means antagonistic. It is, however, an acknowledgment that we who love the church and make our life therein are under an obligation to practice a rigorous self-critique. We are responsible for establishing among ourselves and extending to others reconciliation and relationship with the loving, giving God. We are further charged with maintaining and nurturing this living relationship in a vibrant and living community we call "the church." But a *living* community is of necessity ever-changing, ever-reforming in relationship with and response to a living, giving God. Whenever and wherever we attempt to limit or control access to — or egress from — that community of relationship, by sacramental means in baptism, access to the Eucharist, or the manipulation of penitential rites, I get suspicious, concerned that we are arrogantly assuming more than God allows.

Thus, as balance, I hold in mind and heart the assertion attributed to Jesus in John's gospel: "I am the gate. Whoever enters by me will be saved, and will come in *and go out* and find pasture" (John 10:9, emphasis mine). Such free passage accords with the generosity of a God who will not compel us to love, and the dynamics of living relationship that recognize the nature of love lived and shared between creatures; love waxes and wanes, and must be daily, even momentarily, chosen by each partner.

Bearing the church in suspicion is only another expression of the vigilance demanded of each of us to be constantly aware of our tendency to choose ourselves and our own self-interest over others, our neighbors, and consequently, over God. Suspicion is a right humility, and a preventative against any tendency that would idolize the church, confuse this means to relationship with God and render it an end in itself. With that suspicion in mind and heart, we turn next to the other sacrament central to life in the church: Eucharist.

16

At Table

WHICH CAME FIRST, church or eucharist? Like the puzzle of chicken and egg, this one is not always easy to answer. I favor *eucharist*, uncapitalized—the Greek word for "gratitude, thanks." The Christian gospels are written accounts subsequent to the experience of Jesus. Like Genesis before them, they attempt to make meaning of the disparate experiences of diverse people whose encounter with the Christ, either personally or vicariously through his associates and disciples, deeply touched their lives.

My favorite Easter story is the one told in Luke's gospel of Cleopas and his companion on the road to Emmaus (Luke 24:13ff.). By the time Luke's gospel was written, the church had been around for a while, perhaps a full generation. The story of Cleopas and his companion had probably been told many times. But why was this story chosen, and what prompted the author of the gospel to put this story here?

Was it really to tell us something—anything—about the resurrection? Was it really included as a historical narrative of supposed eyewitnesses to the resurrected Jesus? Or was there some other purpose for sharing this story with a Christian community with some years on it?

I believe one purpose of the story is revealed in the phrase, "but something kept them from seeing who it was." That was a rather important issue for the early church. Uppermost in many minds was the question of how anyone could encounter Jesus, and certainly how anyone could encounter the resurrected Jesus, and be oblivious? Why were they so clueless? It was an important question then and it remains an important question now.

What kept Cleopas and his companion from seeing who it was who walked with them? Was it their intimacy that precluded their revelation? They were obviously close, these two, and they were certainly focused on the matters at hand. They'd been caught up in a rather impressive series of events. And, from what they disclose about themselves, they considered themselves followers of Jesus. "We had hoped that he was the one to liberate Israel," they confessed.

When Jesus comes upon them, they're deep in conversation. When Jesus asks them what they're discussing, the faces they turn to him are sad. They are grieving, absorbed by their sadness. Hurt and confused by what they have experienced, they've withdrawn into themselves. They're struggling to make sense of so much that they don't understand, so much that has turned their world upside down and left them confused.

They'd been hoping for a new life, and they'd probably been planning for it. They'd begun to see themselves and their world in a new way. Then the old world and its ways intervened, and suddenly, they were back where they'd started, going home to Emmaus. But they were returning confused, wondering what had happened and how it had happened and why it had happened. Sadness and grief often accompany a radical disorientation in our lives.

Walking along the road together, Cleopas and his companion were the very picture of closeness, intimately bound to one another in their disappointment, tightly bonded in their mutual concern and pain. They were on an open road, but they were inwardly oriented.

That's what kept them from seeing, I suspect. They couldn't see beyond themselves. Every exchange in their meeting with the unrecognized Jesus is self-oriented. They're frankly amazed that he knows nothing of what they've suffered, taken aback that he's so ignorant of the events that have made them sad. Even when they tell the story of what's happened, they tell it as personal disappointment. When they speak of Jesus, it's as if his own suffering and death are but an accessory to their own.

Cleopas and his companion offer us a window into the church in the time of Luke's gospel, a church preoccupied with its own survival and perpetually sad in its disappointments, a church old enough to have run out of hope for a literal Second Coming of Jesus, yet young enough to have known that hope. It's a church old enough to have known persecution, but young enough to have known the vigor of resistance. It's a church old enough to know diversity, yet young enough to remember homogeneity. It's a church old enough to be tired, but young enough to recall its energy. And it's a church consumed with itself. Deep in conversation, and deeply concerned about itself, it's a church moving rapidly toward stolid institutionalization.

Cleopas and his companion don't welcome the stranger into their conversation; Jesus has to insinuate himself into their meditation. When he offers them questions, they reveal their preoccupation with their own concerns. When they remain introverted, he rebukes them, but they're strangely passive. Even a mild insult from a stranger doesn't slap them from their stupor, and even after he retells the story of Israel's history, they remain self-centered. When he makes to leave them, they beg him to stay, not of any desire to offer him hospitality but rather that they not be left alone.

Cleopas and his companion, the church they represent, the church we can become and are always in danger of becoming, are all as constricting and formidable as the rock-hewn tomb. Hospitality isn't what we offer others nearly so often or enjoy so well as what we give to ourselves.

That's why the dinner in Emmaus is so important. The eucharist at the table of Cleopas and his companion is the strangest of all communions. In our eucharist, we pray fervently that Jesus be with us in the bread and the wine, that Jesus come. We pray that the bread and wine become his body and his blood, that he might abide with us and live in us. We pray that Jesus be present to us and that this meal be central to who and what we are. But as soon as the bread is broken in Emmaus, Jesus disappears. He's gone. The bread is only bread. And they are left alone.

Jesus won't be bound by their intimacy. He won't be entombed in their sad preoccupation with themselves. Jesus wants nothing to do with their community. He leaves them. As he breaks bread, as their eyes open, he vanishes. It's all one simultaneous act.

They're shattered all over again. At the end of this terrible day, in the safety of their own home, in the security of their own table, in the middle of the dark night, Cleopas and his companion are shattered all over again. But this time they don't implode, shattering inward. They explode and shatter outward. Despite the darkness and the hour and the distance they've covered emotionally and physically, they burst out of that warm home, leaving their half-eaten dinner, and they rush back to Jerusalem to tell their story. They go to tell the story every Christian learns by heart, and is commissioned to tell until, by God's grace, we get it right.

This powerful story gets the sequence right, I think. The gratitude, the awareness of indebtedness, of reliance upon another comes at table. The table is such a strange place, yet so common. Strange, for the table is associated with and reserved for intimacy. It's a place of trust. Seated at table, one is vulnerable. The table is literally dangerous; the guard is down, the hands occupied, the attention averted. One could be ambushed, or poisoned. Moreover, eating is socially risky, a rather foolish and embarrassing business. Even dressed up and decorated to the hilt, putting food in one's mouth is ungainly, the process of chewing and swallowing distorts, contorts our features. Therefore, we tended at least until relatively late, to reserve eating to private, and usually among family and only close friends; invitation to dine was high honor.

But another vulnerability is unmasked at table. As we take food into our bodies, we capitulate to our dependency upon this earth to sustain us. We are not perpetual motion machines. Our lives depend upon a cycle of abundance beyond our controlling, a reality far more palpable to our ancestors perhaps than to us, but a reality still. Deprived of food and water, we perish; and to starve to death, or to be starved to death, is still the most gruesome and feared demise imaginable.

I was very early taught the eucharistic sequence, not at church but at my Sicilian grandparents' table. Gathered at a round table that acknowledged no "head" and offered ample capacity for accommodating one more, we sat down to eat in the kitchen of their modest company-built home in a little coal-mining town in the hills of western Pennsylvania, a home that was their refuge from a Sicilian poverty so dire as to make this humble rung so near the bottom of the American socioeconomic ladder a generous improvement. At that table my grandmother took into her hands the crusty loaf she had labored hard to make and bake. As she cradled the bread, her thumb gently traced the sign of the cross on the brown surface, her secret prayer offered for it all—for the flour and yeast, for the sheltering warmth, and for the spouse, children, and grandchildren fed and nurtured by the God whose abundance, so evident in her life, filled her heart with gratitude.

My benignly curmudgeonly grandfather was less demonstrative in his faith, but his ceremonial pouring of his own homemade wine from an old decanter and his glass raised in salute simultaneously thanked God and invoked good health and long life upon us all. That health and life were evidenced in abundant food, laughter, and endless stories connecting our lives to a host of others, some scattered across this country, others separated by an ocean and some even by death itself. But in those gestures and moments, within that sacred space, all came to life and shared the hospitality of that circle.

Tradition says that the author of Luke's gospel—the only one recounting the story of Cleopas, his companion, the road to Emmaus, and the eucharistic revelation at table—also gave us the account of Pentecost in the Acts of the Apostles (Acts 2). While the story neglects to say so, surely there was food on that occasion. Only at table, sharing their enthusiastic stories with one another, could our ancestors have discerned a connection with that distant meal where, gathered with his disciples for the Passover meal in a room set apart, Jesus adjured them to remember him at table.

Commanded by the Christ for the continual remembrance of his life, death, and resurrection until his coming again, the sacramental meal is itself a shared creation, a powerful collaboration between the Christ and his community, the church. I have no doubt of Jesus' commendation that any future remembrance of him be at table; it is fully consistent with all that he was and wished his followers to be.

Remembrance is a many-dimensioned word. Christians have long debated its meaning in the Eucharist. The word demands a generosity allowing the interplay of its varied meanings. Like a sacrament itself, the word's complexities allow entry and engagement at many points.

To remember is, as its most common definition says, to call to mind. And mindfulness is certainly a desirable aspect to bring to any sacrament. If, indeed, a sacrament is a discipline or practice—in the case of Christian practice and discipline, an intentional entering of one's relationship with God—then a mindful attentiveness to the other is no less essential to this relationship than to any of the host of relationships we know and value. We cannot be present to the other if our attention is distracted, if we are not truly mind-ful, have our minds full of and completely attuned to the other in that moment.

But remembrance has a tangible, incarnate dimension, as well. To "re-member" is to reassemble, to put back together something that has been broken, fragmented, or separated. Thus when Jesus tells the disciples at the Last Supper that to gather at table is how they are to "re-member" him, how they can "re-member" him, he is inviting them into an eternal incarnation and radical resurrection.

At table, they shall be reminded of their own vulnerability and dependency and they shall be moved to gratitude. At table, they shall become as he is: vulnerable, dependent upon God, thankful. At table, they practice a sacrifice of praise and thanksgiving—re-membering, reincarnating the sacrifice of Christ, whose own vulnerability, dependency, and gratitude are made present, and they practice becoming one with him in his offering of himself in this radical practice of generous living and prodigal self-giving.

The Holy Eucharist, variously called the Lord's Supper, Holy Communion, the Divine Liturgy, the Mass, and the Great Offering, is at heart always the same practice: being at table. That ritual table is always set with bread and wine, tangible and visible elements present at the table of that first Eucharist and Last Supper, given and received according to Christ's command. Shared at table, these very real and symbolic elements link those at table with the table of origin, and with every table provisioned by the generous hand of God, who gives the wheat and grape, and the time and talent that convert each into sustenance and joy.

I have drawn upon the image of my paternal grandparents' table, but I was also sacramentally shaped by my maternal family, whose traditions were steeped in the life of rural North Carolina. Life in that family was punctuated by Sunday afternoon dinners, at the center of which was a large table spread with the different dishes created and shared by all the women. Full communion entailed sampling at least a taste of every offering, and full inclusion was practiced in a ritual now familiar to many congregations. Any relative incapacitated and thus absent from table was remembered (and re-membered) when someone "fixed a plate" for the missing one. A bit of each food was gathered on a plate and covered with foil or a dish towel, depending upon the distance to be carried, and dispatched to the one who could not be present. In this way, though segregated by infirmity or necessity of labor, that member too was included in the communion of the table, much as bread and wine are now carried from many an altar by ministers designated to bring them to the sick and shut-in.

When death intervened, the same ritual was followed, the only difference being the addition of the coffin, as the deceased was brought home one last time. An abundant table was set and those called to gather for this, the deceased's last act of earthly hospitality, shared the proffered food and wonderful stories. Extreme emotion manifest in tearful grief and eye-watering hilarity, tables and plates laden with food, rooms filled to overflowing with family, friends, and neighbors—all combined to make such events a breathtaking offering of abundance in the midst of a community familiar with hardship and scarcity, and now mourning the loss of life itself. Yet these occasions made real for me the benefits claimed of the Holy Eucharist: the forgiveness of sins, the strengthening of our union with the Christ and one another, and the foretaste of the heavenly banquet which is our nourishment in eternal life.

My maternal grandfather was a moody, taciturn man. A tobacco farmer accustomed to hard work, his impatience with me, his bookish and effete grandson, was rarely hid. Ours was a prickly relationship and in his company I was seldom comfortable, rendering whatever opportunity for communion hopelessly lost. Until my grandfather accidentally slipped and pulled the gas-powered rotary lawnmower over his foot, severing his big toe. The accident left him temporarily grounded.

But I was his eldest grandchild, and the only one with a brand new but valid driver's license. I was entrusted with the keys to his beloved 1956 two-tone turquoise and white Chevrolet Bel Air, and together we went wherever he needed or wanted to go. Conversation remained strained, so I gave in to the silence, content simply to share the time and revel in the sheer joy of driving that car.

Biding my time one warm lazy afternoon, lest Grandaddy want or need a ride, I sat at the untuned upright piano in his living room and plunked out a tune. He was seated just around the corner on the porch, where he visited with an old friend. I wasn't really listening, until I heard him acknowledge the source of the music, saying to his visitor, "That's my grandson, Frances' oldest boy. Plays that thing pretty good, doesn't he?"

Some months later, a massive heart attack—his third—felled him. I was unprepared for the loss, and for the depth of my grief. When I could recover my composure sufficient to bear my self-conscious teenage self publicly, I walked the few yards from our house to his, where his coffin stood open in the living room, family and friends milling about in knots scattered through the house and out in the yard. I drifted from one to another, listening to the stories of my grandfather, reminiscences that confirmed my own assessment of his emotional hardness, a trait he shared with all his brothers. But I also heard the funny stories, the jokes played upon him and those he played on others, and I heard the tales of his generosity, as quiet as the man himself.

As I reflect now upon the experience, I see the very qualities required of Christian Eucharist: examination of our lives, repenting of our sins, and love and charity for all people. In that experience of my late childhood as I stood on the threshold of adulthood, my grief and my grandfather's funeral were my tutor. I came finally to see myself as my grandfather saw me, a beloved grandson. I let go my resentment of him in the full realization of his love for me, a love that loved me for what I was despite my perceived failure to fulfill whatever it was I thought he wanted in a grandson. In his living room, in the presence of his lifeless body, surrounded by all he had built, the life he and my grandmother had made together in that house, with that family, among those friends, I knew what it was to *be* in love and charity.

That's an important nuance deserving note: the requirement of eucharistic communion is not that I love, but that I *be*—that I dwell, that I exist—in love, that I believe myself to be held in love and in charity, that I be aware of and acknowledge the abundance of love and grace I am privileged to know, within which I am blessed to live. Only in this awareness can I be genuinely, humbly *grateful* for this unwarranted, unearned abundance. Only then may I come to God's table appreciative that it is of God's goodness and generosity that I have my place there, and not of any performance or deserving on my part.

But there is one thing more to tell of my grandfather's wake. As the afternoon wore on there came a moment when a ripple moved through the house. Word was being passed that my grandfather's elder, invalid brother was en route. The house quieted and nearly everyone jockeyed for a place in the now-crowded living room, spilling over into every cranny affording even a modest view of the primary space around the coffin. From where I stood in a privileged spot near the foot of the coffin, I could see out the open front door. I saw Uncle Will making his way slowly down the walk, attended on either side. After a long while, he made it to the coffin, upon which he rested his hand to steady himself. For a long time Uncle Will stood silent, gazing down at his deceased brother. Then, in a very quiet but steady voice he said simply, "Goodbye, Charles. I'll be seeing you soon."

With such simple eloquence the power of Resurrection faith passes from generation to generation, without aid of complex theological debate or elaborate liturgical choreography, as it has for centuries, for millennia. For the pattern of life itself is eucharistic, as Jesus well knew when he took bread and wine in hand and bid his disciples remember him. Neither Jesus nor the church "invented" the Eucharist; Eucharist is inherent in the creation. It is deeply embedded in a creation that derives its life only from God, and creatures who, as they come to every meal, come to the vulnerable reality of their own fragility and dependence upon the Other, the one Who made them, loves them, keeps them — the great shepherd who feeds and guards their very life.

Yet that embedded Eucharist lies in and beneath our earth, our life. Hidden by our arrogance and prideful assumption, we fail to see this Eucharist each and every time we come to table without gratitude. We who come to table in the presumption of entitlement, believing this abundance spread before us is our right, accepting it as our due, cannot see the Eucharist for our own blindness. We who come to the table in the pride of accomplishment, believing the bounty set for us is the fruit of our own hands, the recompense of our labor, craft, and ingenuity, are similarly myopic.

Therefore the eucharistic commandment of the Christ is itself a call to mission, a call to make visible that which is too easily obscured. We celebrate the Eucharist in every act of eucharist—every overt acknowledgment of gratitude for God's lavish generosity. Eucharist is thanksgiving, and giving thanks is always eucharist. Eucharist is response to a generosity and love that precedes our gratitude, the church's expression of gratitude for the life it discovered in Pentecost, in the perpetual Pentecosts of life manifest in every union within us, between us, among us, discovered in and through the Christ.

An expression of that gratitude is the continual practice of Eucharist, the practice of being the people of God. This sacrament of Eucharist is a "making believe," an acting out of what we profess to believe of ourselves, of our neighbors, of God. We gather to practice, as the musician takes up his instrument or the athlete her equipment, to run our scales and drills in anticipation of all that is yet to be, in this life and in the life to come.

We gather at the altar, stand at God's table in all our diversity, bearing all our variety and the brokenness and estrangement of that difference. We bring all that to God's table, for it is what God has given each of us and it is all we have truly to offer. Gathered at a table we have not set for ourselves, we are grateful for the bread and wine. We are grateful for the Christ who is our bread, our wine. And for one brief moment, in that shared dependency of hand uplifted and filled, we know our union. In that fleeting and yet eternal moment, we are the Christ, re-membered. He lives in us, and we in him.

In that practice, that radical ritual act, we bring the hidden inherent Eucharist into the light, we make public the essential gratitude of a world for its maker, all creatures for their Creator. We unmask human ambition and pretension, and confess our complicity in the same, daring ourselves and our world to stand in the presence of the humbling, humiliating truth of our utter dependence. We bring forth from earth's tomb as surely as God brought forth Jesus from behind the rock, the truth our impulses deny, the life that is beyond our control. We practice the life of pure gratitude that is the Christ, the life that lives in and through the Spirit, the life that is the Light never overcome, never overpowered by any darkness.

In this tender, tentative meal we experience the fellowship of the saints, we anticipate the heavenly banquet. We gaze silent upon the One who has preceded us, now present and delivered into our hands. We lift bread and wine to our lips, and eat. We are filled and fed. We gaze silently, gratefully upon the One who has preceded us, now present in, with, and among us. And with all that we are and all that we have, we affirm that we shall see him again, soon.

17

As Each Is Called

OTHER SACRAMENTAL RITES evolved in the church, the product of life in relationship with God. They include Confirmation, Ordination, and Holy Matrimony, each of which is a specific response to vocation, the ordering of one's life and commitment in conformity with the demands of particular relationship. Two other rites, Reconciliation of a Penitent and Unction, complete the list of five "minor," or elective, sacraments, so called because unlike Baptism and Eucharist they lack any direct scriptural ordinance attributable to Jesus.

Moreover, these five rites conform to an Anglican formula that identifies them as "available to all, beneficial to some, and required of none." As such, they are not deemed essential for all persons in the same way that Baptism and Eucharist are.

A residual of infant baptism, Confirmation is the rite in which a person who has been previously baptized may express a mature commitment to Christ, and receive strength from the Holy Spirit through prayer and the laying on of hands by a bishop. Prior baptism, instruction in the Christian faith, penitence for sins, and readiness to affirm one's confession of Jesus Christ as Savior and Lord are the requirements for this rite which essentially repeats the affirmations and promises of the baptismal covenant.

While infant baptism is still widely practiced, many parents defer the rite or neglect it entirely, to the end that more Americans today reach adolescence or even adulthood never having experienced that sacrament. When baptism is undertaken at a later age and the candidate is *chrismated*—that is, has the post-baptismal sign of the cross inscribed by a bishop (or in some traditions, a bishop's delegate) on the forehead in holy oil (*BCP*, p. 308)—Confirmation is redundant.

Still, Confirmation is for some a means of personalizing and contemporizing an earlier baptismal covenant undertaken under circumstances lacking full volition. To the extent that it serves this purpose, it can be a powerful signification of a person's dedication to a life of faith. The bishop's laying on of hands is the sign at the center of this rite. While the waters of baptism and the signing (with or without oil) of the newly baptized signify passage into new life and new community, in Confirmation it is the imposition of the bishop's hands that confer passage and welcome to renewed life.

The laying on of episcopal hands in Confirmation and Ordination also signifies the bestowal of the sevenfold gifts of the Holy Spirit, derived from Isaiah 11:2 and variously listed as wisdom, understanding, counsel, might or fortitude, knowledge, godliness or piety, and fear or respectful awe of God. These gifts are offered not just for the benefit of the individual confirmand (or ordinand) but for the good of all; they are bestowed as gifts shared out of God's abundance and are intended to be shared, in turn, by each and all of the faithful, as expressions of God's bounty and generosity.

In some ritual traditions it is also the custom of the bishop to administer the *buffet*, a fairly smart slap to the candidate's cheek, and to proffer the episcopal signet ring for the candidate's lips. These ceremonial additions have largely disappeared, but could be redeemed as tangible reminders of the realities and responsibilities of this passage.

While the buffet was intended to remind the confirmand that the life of faith is no harbor from the world's blows, the fact that the slap is administered by the bishop—who throughout this rite is the very embodiment of the institutional community of the church—is further reminder that neither is the church safe haven from hurt; it's a fallen world, and the church is part of that disordered creation. And while in some instances the episcopal signet ring was/is extended in expectation of the confirmand's respectful kiss, signifying obedience, I have noted bishops who instead actually press the ring to the lips of the kneeling confirmand, thus bestowing a seal of responsibility not unlike the hot coal pressed to the prophet's lips (Isaiah 6:6–7) and commissioning the newly confirmed to use his or her gifts to proclaim the good news of God.

Just as Confirmation is a rite of individual affirmation of baptismal life and responsibility, so Ordination is the rite in which authority and grace are extended to those being made bishops, priests, and deacons through prayer and the laying on of hands by bishops. As the word *ordination* implies, these are rites pertaining to the several meanings of *order*.

The several offices of ministry and leadership in the church have been previously defined and discussed. Laity, bishops, priests, and deacons have defined roles and relationships that are intended to impose some order on the life of the human community and institution called the church. The various rites of Ordination define and establish those roles and relationships.

Baptism is, of course, the primary rite of Ordination belonging to all Christians and is thus the rite conferring the responsibilities of ministry to the lay order. Life in community entails a distribution of specific responsibilities through the gift of relationship. In the active sharing of life in community, one person's need often elicits another person's gifts in response. The recognition of each person's gifts leads to a gradual distribution of the same. When a person consistently evidences gifts specific to ordained ministry as deacon, priest, or bishop, a community may encourage that person to offer themselves for that work in the church.

Vocation, from the Latin word for "call," or "summons," is a central dynamic of a faithful life. The lifelong search for meaning and purpose in a believer's life is deeply rooted in relationship with God. The lifelong "conversation" with God, which often seems one-sided and terribly quiet to the casual observer, can actually be quite animated and not a little quarrelsome. In any intimate relationship words are seldom the only, or even the most prevalent, medium of communication. In the deep and abiding relationships of our lives we develop a more subtle language, one that relies on old habit, subtle intimations, and nuanced perceptions.

To say that one has "heard" or "responded" to a "call" draws confused responses from those whose minds tend toward the literal and can only imagine disembodied voices now manageable with pharmaceuticals, or arcane signs appearing in the luncheon tortilla. Would that vocation were so simply or quickly discerned. For most of us, it's a lifetime of thoughtful, observant paying attention to the patterns of daily living.

My dear Catholic aunt loves to point to a photo taken of me near my first birthday in which my chubby little hands are raised in what appears to be the classic position of the celebrant standing over bread and wine at the altar and declare, "See, I just *knew* you were going to be a priest!" What was seemingly so vividly obvious to her was a lot longer in reaching clarity for *me*.

Like many a child, I imagined myself in many different roles, changing my mind many times a day. As I grew older, facilities in language, art, and music emerged while it became abundantly clear that I would never excel at any sport or any profession demanding any math higher than long division. College experience as a dormitory resident advisor and summer camp administrator revealed unexpected abilities, and the combination of a war in Southeast Asia, a low draft lottery number, and the cancellation of most graduate study deferments for military service all conspired to clarify my own call to ministry. In short, ministry had never crossed my mind until the day I first heard myself say to an understanding Episcopal rector, "I think I want to be a priest."

If that sounds tentative, it should. It was my first halting step in a process of discernment, which is to say I offered myself to the possibility of ordained ministry, the institutional community that disciplines, shapes, and orders that ministry, and the community it serves. Very quickly I learned that such offering means turning one's life over to the scrutiny of others. Thus began the first stage of discernment, which is given to assessing a person's fitness for this work. I was subjected to a variety of tests and interviews aimed at evaluating me and my gifts. Did I have sufficient education, experience, and maturity? Were there sufficient foundations to support me and all entrusted to me in the process and the ministry that might proceed from it?

For my part, I began watching and listening more attentively both to what I heard myself saying and doing, and to the responses elicited from others. I began to see more clearly how the several abilities evidenced in my life—language, music, counsel, administration—found affirmation from others. And I learned to pay attention to my being— to who I am, "just as I am," as an old hymn says it, and to the responses of others to all that I am. I began to see more clearly and honestly all that was valued, all in need of correction, and all that was forgiven. Over a period of years that included seminary and extended beyond, I gradually passed from the stage of fitness to the longer and subtler stage of readiness. In my case, that readiness did not come till nearly two years past the awarding of my seminary degree, at which time I was able to say to my bishop, I believe I am ready, if the church is ready.

The vocational sacraments are rites of self-giving gift giving. There is no "right" to ordination, or to matrimony. Nor are the rites of these sacraments about "rights" incurring to those who stand at the center of the action—the ordinand in ordination, or the pair being wed in holy matrimony. On these occasions, in these rites, persons are offering their lives to God and to God's people. In ordination the gift is to the whole church but also to a specific community, congregation, ministry, or diocese; in matrimony the gift is one person to another, and of both to the larger community present and to the world beyond.

The community of the church reserves to itself the decision to defer, accept, or reject the gift offered. The church may not have perceived my gifts as consonant with the church's need or utility. The church may have deemed me unfit for this work, or unready for service. Of any couple seeking Holy Matrimony, the church may determine the gift of that relationship inappropriate, unfit, or even harmful. Thus no bishop can ever be compelled to ordain, nor can any priest be compelled to officiate at a wedding.

While there is no "right" to any vocational sacrament, the celebration of these rites within the church incurs responsibilities for all involved, as in all giving and receiving of gifts. The giver surrenders the gift, releases and entrusts it to the recipient. There is then something unconditional in each of these vocational offerings, but there is also in each of these gifts a mutuality. Thus the ordinand, and in Matrimony the couple, accept both responsibility and privilege. They accept responsibility for a life of continual giving of self daily to God and to the other(s) in community.

The community meets this gift of trust with the mutual gift of *privilege*, which means literally "private law," or perhaps more commonly, a trust of privacy protected even by civil law. For example, no clergyperson can be compelled by law to reveal information shared and sealed by confession; neither can any intrude upon the intimacies shared by married partners.

If God intends for all humans a meaningful, purposeful life, how are the Christian's sexual relations to be integrated into that vocation? Furthermore, because that vocation is not only a personal matter, but also a social or communal one, how is the Christian to mediate sexual relations between those private and public dimensions?

Christians believe that all are called to personal relationship with God and to particular relationship in the world—some to union with one person, some to celibacy. Holy Matrimony is the sacramental rite of Christian marriage, in which by common and classical definition a woman and man enter into a lifelong union, in vows before God and the church, asking and receiving the grace and blessing of God to help them fulfill their vows.

The church has traditionally taught that in the sacrament of marriage the individuals making their promises are the celebrants of the sacrament. The rest of the assembly—including the priest—are witnesses. People have married and given themselves in commitment to one another far longer than sacramental forms have existed. Sacramentalizing such giving is an expression of the couple's and the church's willingness to share the gift of relationship. The couple invites the church to participate in their love, and the church accepts the couple's relationship as part of the community's corporate witness. Thus the couple benefits from the support and nurture of the church community that understands and upholds their intention to live in love and fidelity, and the church is beneficiary of the couple's gift of covenant love.

In undertaking this covenant commitment within the particular community of the church, a couple is asking the community to share responsibility for keeping and nurturing that commitment. While it has been argued that in the cases of any marriages subsequent to divorce and of same-sex unions the church ought not accept such responsibility, the refusal of this invitation demands serious examination. Those who choose to live out their commitments may need us and the support of our community, as we insistently maintain; but that is only half the story. The other half is that we have need of them.

Some divorced and some homosexual Christians desire to share their commitment with a larger community. The church articulates its expectations in the vows within the marriage rite, the only portion of the rite that is unalterable. The Christian marital vows do specify monogamy. Monogamy literally means only "one marriage," posing a challenge to our altering the word to mean "one marriage *at a time*." In modern usage monogamy is redefined as commitment to a single partner.

But fidelity is not limited only to genital exclusivity; it extends to every aspect of the commitment. Nor is genital activity a prerequisite to consummation; pledging vows alone suffices to consummate the covenant promise. That the private exercise of this commitment may or may not include genital intimacy is of no concern to the community of the church.

The Christian community deems promiscuity, exploitation, abuse, and violence as destructive behaviors inconsistent with love, and adulterations of the covenant vows that challenge the promise of the community to uphold these two persons in their vows. But the community is also invited to consider fidelity, respect, nurture, and affection as constructive behaviors and exemplary expressions of covenant love. Such virtues encourage the promise of the community to uphold these two persons in their vows and confirm the promises of the individuals to so live within community as to enrich rather than impoverish it.

Technically, Christian women and men do not need the church's permission to commit their lives to one another, as demonstrated by the church's respect for and recognition of civil marriage. But neither can any partners expect the unequivocal or uncritical acceptance of their relationship within the church; membership in the community of the faithful invites continuous confession and repentance and the critical ministrations of the whole. Those moved to offer their relationship, even to the pain that inevitably comes of living in community, are making a gift to the church. As such, they contribute to the church's own vocation, challenging the church to discern God's call in their offering. The church's response to the proffered gift reflects not the quality of the giver or the gift, but the grace, or lack thereof, of the church itself—for the church also stands in need of repentance and within God's critical considerations.

All Christians are encouraged to take their place in the church and to offer with perseverance the gift of their love, and their covenant relationships. The church is challenged and encouraged to receive that gift with gratitude, remembering that we are commanded to be thankful in all things, even those gifts we do not understand or do not receive to our perceived comfort or benefit.

The blessing of marriage invoked and proclaimed by the church affirms God's presence in the particular commitment of one person to another, and the intention of those so joined to live into that presence and promise such that their relationship might be a sign to this broken world, a vehicle incarnating the presence of God to others. At the heart of it, any blessing is a form of creedal affirmation, affirmation that there is no place where God is not. We bless infants and children—once considered outcast, or at the least, second class—in affirmation that God is present in and for the child. We bless the sick and dying who were once, and sadly sometimes are still, abandoned and devalued, affirming that God is present in and to human suffering, and even death itself.

Blessing is neither permission nor sanction of behavior. It is proclamation and promise of God's presence and possibility. The blessing of military troops and armaments is neither permission nor sanction to do war; it is proclamation and promise of God's presence even in the midst of human sin and strife, and the possibility of God's redemptive power to transform our tragedy. After all, Christians do not bless bread and wine, proclaiming body and blood in token that we should practice human sacrifice (a charge once leveled against Christians by those who did not understand our rites), but rather to affirm that even in our darkest hour and most vicious transgression—the passion and death of Jesus—God did not abandon us, but was and always is fully present.

Nor is blessing preventive of sin. Absolution does not render us sinless, nor does baptism ensure that we shall live in perfection. What we bless in any human commitment is promise—intention. We say as much in an invitation to confession extended to all who "intend to lead a new life" (*BCP*, p. 330). God is present in the promise, in the intention.

Thus, in the blessing of marriage, we affirm the promise to live in love and commitment, even though we know full well and acknowledge in our wedding prayers, that each partner will hurt the other in the failure to fulfill the promise. We pray not *if* they hurt each other, but *when* they hurt each other, they shall reaffirm and return to God's presence, seek God's pardon (and each other's), and reconcile (*BCP*, p. 330). The blessing of marriage proclaims that there is no place where God is not—proclamation that gives us the heart to risk our love in intimate trust, and to repent our abuses and be healed of any abuses we suffer. That proclamation is genderless, applicable to any and all human commitment.

If and when the church blesses same-sex union, it may be that we are approaching a challenge anticipated by Jesus (despite the lament that in so doing we are losing our values and our morals, not to mention our minds). In his radical redefinition of the family, Jesus anticipates a culture much like our own, where traditional kinships and loyalties are more diverse (Matthew 12:46–50; Mark 3:31–35; Luke 8:19–21). Jesus maintains that family and kinship transcend blood and biology, that the basis of union is neither gender nor generativity, but promise. Jesus opens the possibility for blessing and affirming the presence of God in a wide variety of human commitment, including but not limited to heterosexual marriage. Jesus opens the possibility for blessing and affirming same-sex commitments, childless heterosexual marriages, and even single-parent households.

We acknowledge as holy every evidence of God present in human commitment and love and we expressly challenge couples in the marriage prayers to "make their life together a sign of Christ's love to this sinful and broken world, that unity may overcome estrangement, forgiveness heal guilt, and joy conquer despair" (*BCP*, p. 429). We affirm the reality of God's active presence in every human promise of love, God's loving desire to receive all love as gift, God's promise to be present to all who seek God's assistance in the keeping of commitment, and God's pardon of every failure encountered along the way. We encourage one another, and the world around us, with the constant proclamation in word and deed that there is no place where God is not.

The church, like each of its members, is daily challenged by the gospel's indiscriminate inclusion. Though we proclaim a desire and duty to extend the gospel in wider witness, obligating us to be more inclusive, we have never quite resolved the prodigal nature of a gospel that extends itself even to those we consider our enemies. If we value what we have learned of God in our own committed relationships, is that not a gift worthy of sharing? And if evangelism means extending what we have learned of God, including what we learn of God in intimacy, is this not something we can share? Respecting the dignity of every human, being a component of our baptismal covenant, includes respecting each person's response to God's call to relationship. Christians appropriately ask of one another: How do you perceive God's call in your life, and what graces have you discerned in relation to that call? But we must be prepared to receive replies that challenge our own assumptions, that open us—as all conversation does—to the possibility of change, and to deeper, vaster experience of the boundless love of God.

18

When Love
Draws Close

ALL THE SACRAMENTS considered thus far share in common a very public expression. They are rites intended to be experienced within the full assembly of a congregation, that congregation itself representing the entire people of God. But there are moments in one's life when so public a venue is neither desirable nor practicable. Those moments demand a more intimate expression of active relationship with God, and with God's people. They include the very private matters of personal contrition and penitence, of profound illness and the threshold of death. For such moments, the church offers the sacramental rites of reconciliation and unction.

I preface consideration of these "intimate sacraments" with a digression on the word *parson*. This quaint and archaic corruption of the English word *person* seems uniquely suited to the role of the lay or clergy pastor administering the intimate sacraments. The parson is the person who embodies the whole community of God's faithful family; he or she is that person who is personally associated with, authorized by, and identified with a specific congregation. The nagging insistence of the hospitalized or housebound person that "the rector" be the one to make a visit is simply saying they want the *parson* with them. While that person may, indeed, be the rector, the principle deserves consideration. The parson, then, whether ordained or lay, is the one in whose person a whole congregation may attend and be present to an individual whose circumstances demand and deserve privacy.

Nearly every sacramental rite offers some opportunity for general confession, when those gathered give voice to the reality of failure and brokenness common to human life. *The Book of Common Prayer* is filled with confessions—within all the orders for corporate and personal prayer offices, the eucharistic rites and optional penitential orders prefacing them, embedded within the various forms of the prayers of the people, and appended in seasonal collects and "additional prayers." Extended amplification of and emphasis upon the role of confession are evidenced in a general exhortation (p. 316) available for use on any occasion, and in an exhortation and litany of penitence in the rite for Ash Wednesday, which ushers in the season of Lent, and the Great Litany, which is often used on the first Sunday commencing the semi-penitential season of Advent. These general confessions usually acknowledge not only those sins and offenses of which one is mindful, but also all those hurtful and offensive acts one inflicts unknowingly. The open and public expression of these realities is met with a general absolution, an assurance of God's prodigal pardon, voiced by the priest or officiant.

The purpose of these general exercises is not intended to be a casual or wholesale tossing off of the very hurtful, damaging things we do to others or to ourselves. Like all oracular prayer, the open expression of these realities is a device intended to re-mind us. Just as hearing oneself actually articulate the names of the sick or needy may put us in mind actually to reach out in love to those named, so actually hearing oneself acknowledge the ever-present reality of the sinful acts that separate and drive us apart, and that rive, rend, and sabotage our own selves and lives, may re-mind us of specific acts and occasions of sin. The general confession and the accompanying general absolution are not encouragement to slough off sin, but are rather invitation to explore more deeply and honestly the darkness and brokenness of one's own life. The general confession and absolution not only bring our darkness to light, but are also lights with which we arm ourselves for those frightening forays into our own depths. By those lights we are better able to find and face the very specific sources of our pain and brokenness, to name and claim the realities of own fragmentation and separation.

Whether the product of seasonal encouragement, as in Lent or Advent; of professional analysis, spiritual direction, or thoughtful reflection; or the rare but blinding revelation of honest confrontation with reality, having identified the sources of one's own dis-ease, the rite for Reconciliation of a Penitent, or Penance (BCP, pp. 447ff.), is provided the person who repents of specific sin. Following the dictum that this resource is "available to all, beneficial to some, and required of none," the penitent person may confess that sin to God in the presence of another—clergy or lay person—and receive the assurance of pardon and the grace of absolution pronounced by a bishop or priest, or forgiveness declared by a deacon or lay confessor.

Penitence is literally to be sorry, to regret. But what to do with that sorrow, that regret? The public assembly of corporate worship is rarely the appropriate time or place for baring one's innermost soul, much less revealing private acts or behaviors in which other members of the community may be complicit. While, as we shall see, some public action may eventually be called for, other steps may precede it. The ritual form for reconciliation is not a mandatory formulary; confession is valid and acceptable in most any open expression. The rite does, however, provide a template, an order, that can focus and facilitate the process of bringing one's error and wrongdoing into the open, and of seeking and finding reconciliation.

Even the posture of the rite can vary. Some few parish churches still offer the traditional confessional "closet," an enclosed booth with space for a confessor divided by a screen from space for the penitent making confession. In other places, the person hearing confession may sit in a chair inside a chancel, back to the communion rail, while the penitent making confession kneels at the rail to one side, at the confessor's shoulder, following the rite in a quiet voice spoken directly into the confessor's ear. Increasingly, the practice of ritual confession is undertaken face to face, confessor and penitent seated across from one another, either in a small space set apart for this purpose, or in the privacy of the confessor's office or the penitent's home.

Regardless the place or the posture, I find it essential to engage the conversational dimension the rite affords if I, as confessor, am to "offer counsel, direction, and comfort" as the rite allows. While the rite offers the penitent a brief "fill in the blank" for naming the presenting sin, few of us are capable of embracing or articulating our dilemmas so tersely. It is often helpful and instructive to discern just how and why the penitent has arrived at the perception of this act as "sinful."

Moreover, if the object of the rite is true reconciliation, then it is necessary to identify the specific fractures in need of mending. Whose lives are touched by this act of sin? Where is the hurt, the alienation? What can and must be done by the penitent, and others, to restore wholeness? What is beyond our mending, and can we trust God to be and act where we cannot? Such questions, whether answered aloud or pondered privately, frame the hard work of contrition and reconciliation.

The absolution or assurance of God's forgiveness does not obviate a person's responsibility. As the word *responsibility* infers, if one is endowed with the ability to respond, one is under obligation to do so. Thus, the proper acts of contrition and penitence extend beyond merely voicing one's sorrow in private. In very extreme instances, where confession may include illegal or criminal behavior, the confessor's exploration of the aforementioned questions with the penitent can present profound challenges with complex moral and legal consequence, but the usual exercise of these disciplines is more mundane. Still, some general principles pertain.

For example, let's say a penitent comes to me and confesses that she has cheated. While using a friend's computer, she discovered a paper written by her friend for another course and professor, a paper that satisfies the requirements of an assignment she has been given but has neglected to do. She copies the friend's paper to her own disk, makes a few alterations, prints the paper, and turns it in as her own.

Who is harmed? The student who has cheated, the friend from whom she has stolen, and the professor who is responsible for assessing each student's grasp of the matter being taught. Of course, by extension, the circle could be drawn more widely. Should the infraction go unconfessed and undetected, harm extends to all the students in the class whose own hard work has been demeaned and perhaps adversely graded; to the reputation of the university whose respect depends upon the virtue and acumen of its graduates; and to any and all persons whose lives may be injured by this cheating student's moral assumptions and material ignorance.

But let's assume that this sin has been detected and confessed early, that the paper has only been turned in and not yet graded. What can be done? The difficult work of penance might well include confessing the theft to her friend and to the professor, and working through the consequences with each. The assurance of God's forgiveness is encouragement to embrace these hard disciplines and their consequences.

When pronouncing absolution or declaring forgiveness, I lay hands on the penitent's head, sometimes retracing on the forehead the sign of the cross received at baptism and remembered in the seasonal imposition of ashes, or at least take and hold the penitent's hands—to make physical contact—and when appropriate, embrace the penitent in an exchange of peace at the conclusion of the rite. The proclamation of an incarnate God recommends tangible expression in such important moments. It communicates to the penitent that God not only forgives and has forgiven, but that God and God's incarnate presence in God's people will be physically present as the penitent undertakes the very demanding work of reconciliation. With this concrete assurance, the penitent sinner is emboldened to face the discordant music and difficult mechanics that are a part of restoring harmony and reconciling brokenness.

Being a sacrament of intimacy, the rite of reconciliation is undertaken in strict privacy. It is never appropriate for the confessor to discuss any aspect of this exchange outside the intimacy of the confessional relationship and the sealed boundary of the rite. It is appropriate, however, for each person in this intimate rite, as in any relationship, to hold the other fully accountable. Thus, a confessor who indulges abusive, illegal, or inappropriate behavior within this private context has already violated the trust of the community he or she represents as parson, and the trust of the penitent whose dignity (worthiness) the confessor has in baptism pledged to respect as person. But a penitent who indulges abusive, illegal, or inappropriate behavior within this private context violates the trust of the community represented in the parson, and the trust of the confessor whose dignity is also assured in the penitent's baptismal promise.

Issues of human dignity also attend the other intimate rite, Unction of the Sick. *Unction* means "anointing" and is the rite of applying oil and/or the laying hands upon the sick for the healing of spirit, mind, and body. Usually reserved for and associated with extreme illness, unction is the intimate expression of a practice increasingly incorporated into public worship in various healing rites. Just as confession can have a general, public expression, so too may prayer and laying on of hands be part of a congregation's corporate worship. As a component of prayer within the daily office or the Eucharist, or as a discrete service offered on special occasion, these public events serve to restore and re-member the body of God's people. Those able to come forward and those unable to be present except in a representative who bears the absent person to the community's center (thus performing the "parson" role in a different dimension) all gather to receive specific and intentional prayer, and the laying on of hands (with or without oil) for the purpose of healing.

Here it becomes necessary to distinguish between healing and curing. To cure is to rid of disease, to restore to health. To heal means to restore to wholeness. While they may seem indistinguishable, I hold these to be distinctly different functions and ends.

I can never ignore or refute God's power to accomplish anything. Neither can I demand or effect. I recognize that the human condition is mortality itself—that our lives are bounded and limited by time. Our bodies are subject to wear and tear, and to accident and violence. I believe in miracle, which means only "to wonder at." Indeed, by that definition, all life qualifies. But I also subscribe to reality, and the reality of our human being is that we are mortal. Moreover, consistent with my faith in human freedom as the gift of the prodigal God, I do not expect God to contravene my own responsibility, for to do so would be disrespectful of my own human being. That God's ways are not like my ways and that God's bountiful prodigality constantly challenges my own limited expectations fill me with wonder, and my life with miracle.

Much as I might wish to cure or be cured of any mortal wound or fatal disease, that power is not given to me or any other human. That the grace and bounty of medicine and the medical arts may forestall my death, the greatest sadness of human being is that we are ultimately separated—our bodies, relationships, and communities fractured—by death.

But wholeness is another matter. No mortal wound or fatal disease should ever physically separate us prematurely. None of us should ever suffer the living death of isolation, of exile. Throughout his earthly ministry, Jesus was remarkable in his reaching out and over all the barriers that separate, especially those posed by illness. Touching lepers, touching the lips of the speechless, the eyes of the blind, the ears of the deaf, he reconnected those exiled from the human family and re membered the body of God's people on earth. By word and example he commanded his disciples to do the same. He did not have to confer any special power upon them, for this power to heal, to be connected in relationship, is the gift of the abundant God given in creation. Instead, he called them to this responsibility. This power, this ability to establish relationship, allows every human to respond to another. Jesus holds us accountable to this vocation. We need never be separated by hunger, nakedness, or homelessness. We need never be separated by prison. We need never be separated by illness or disease. We have the ability to respond to these deprivations, degradations of human being.

This power was made manifest to me in the days when AIDS was still surrounded by a cloud of unknowing and a fog of misinformation. I visited a student in hospital. Set apart in a private room, the door plastered with warning messages, I declined an exiting nurse's offer of a mask and gloves, and she did not insist. I entered to find the student alone, seated on the edge of his bed, feet hanging limply, his body depleted by pneumonia. He looked up as I entered and in a weak voice warned me of possible contamination. But I drew closer and when I asked if I might sit beside him, he patted the bed. We sat in quiet for a brief while. I slowly raised my arm to encircle his shoulder and when I rested it, he slumped and leaned his head easily into that space between my shoulder and neck, and wept quietly. Few words passed between us, but when I rose to go, our hands joined, he looked into my eyes and said, "Thank you. Thank you for the first time in weeks that I have been touched. Without gloves. Without masks. Just touched." He was not cured, but he had in that moment been healed, restored to community, re-membered among the people of God.

Unction affords opportunity for the community, in its representative parson, to be present to the person whose illness forbids active participation in the congregation's life. But it also allows that community to be present in that intimate moment of extremity as one passes from life through death. Anointing as death draws near reaffirms and reclaims the dying person as one who belongs to God's family, bound in relationship to the community of God's people and not consigned to eternal death. It is a last tangible reminder to the one on the way out of this life and to those who remain that we are all bound together, all gathered up in God's bountiful love and a prodigality even death cannot stanch.

God's activity is neither controlled by nor limited to these rites;

they are ordered practices and disciplines by which the people of God in the church find in material things and physical actions the means and media to give expression to human relationship with God, and God's relationship with us. As such, all sacraments incarnate our faith in God and God's faith in us, express and enliven our love of God and God's love of us, sustain our present hope in God's abiding relationship with us in this life, and anticipate hope's future fulfillment in eternal relationship with God in a life and presence unbounded by death.

19

Ultimate Trust

HOPE IS BOTH A NOUN AND A VERB. As a noun the first and preferred meaning of hope is trust, reliance. It is more than a synonym of faith; it is rather the embodiment of one's trust. When the Christian uses hope as a verb, this essential meaning remains intact. Hope, then, is not—as popularly assumed—a kind of wishing, not even an anticipation. Hope, the verb, is the activity of faith. Christian hope is living with confidence in newness and fullness of life as the abundant gift of a prodigal creative God, with reliance upon the reality of the Christ's promise of God's enduring love manifest in the relationship of Jesus and God, and with trust in the fulfillment of God's purpose for the world evident in and guided by the Spirit.

Christians speak of the coming of Christ in glory. For some, this coming is a definitive and literal reappearance of the resurrected Jesus in whom the fullness of the Christ is revealed, and glory a victorious, vindicating resplendence refuting the suffering and lowly status of Jesus and his first followers. Certainly, the early scriptures of Christian communities perceived such a return and expressed this fervent desire. Yet the militaristic and materialistic dimensions of this perception, while consistent with human impulses, are at odds with the life and teaching of Jesus himself. Scripture, when taken in its entirety, offers evidence that even those closer to Jesus and to the historic events that reveal his fulfillment of the vocation as the Christ perceived this contradiction. The succession of letters attributed to the apostle Paul allows us to see how this anticipation became for him a substantive hope.

As Paul's faith matures and time's trajectory carries his life further from the historical details of Jesus' life and experience, Paul begins to perceive and to speak of the church, God's people, as Christ's body. The coming of Christ in glory becomes for him less a manifest display of God's superlative might and more an incarnate fulfillment of God's loving will for the world. Christ will come, does come, whenever and wherever the body of the resurrected Christ, the church, manifests God's will for human being in wholeness, in abundant mercy and prodigal love. This body, this remarkable wholeness manifesting genuine human integrity, is God's power made incarnate, and does make all things new.

Christian hope is the living of life as Jesus lived it, a life so imbued with trust in God and confidence in God's love and abundance that it manifests, incarnates as does the life of Jesus, the fullness of human being willed by God in creation, evidenced in the Christ, and sustained by the Spirit of that relationship. Jesus assures that he is present wherever two or more are gathered in his name (Matthew 18:20). That assurance is for us not only a promise but a responsibility; we are the inheritors of his life and ministry. We are his body in the world.

But what of life beyond this world and time? What do we mean by heaven and hell? As creatures of time and space, our natural inclination is to perceive heaven and hell in these dimensions. Of the many challenges of ministry, some of the most demanding involve death. I certainly found this so when called home for the funeral of a cousin and her young son. They had been shot by her former husband, she intentionally and the son accidentally, after which the former husband had turned the gun on himself and taken his own life. The circumstances of their deaths left the living in a roiling stew of complex emotions. Pain, anger, remorse, and recrimination abounded. Fears that we might have said or done something—or that we did not say or do something, anything—that could have affected or averted this tragedy. Fear of all our anger—anger at God, at ourselves, at the one who had pulled the trigger, at everyone and anyone who might have done something, anything, to prevent this horror. Fear of an anger so deeply seated within us that it is beyond reason, the kind of irrational anger that only the thinnest veneer of sanity holds in check.

In the midst of this family tragedy, I sought in myself and urged others to compassion for the killer, whose extramarital infidelity and divorce of our cousin had undermined respect for him long before he descended to madness and murder. My grieving sister asked if I believed he was in hell. I answered no. What's hell *for* then? she asked. Perhaps, I replied, so we have a place to put those we can no longer love.

Heaven then becomes the place we put all those whom we cannot cease to love, whom we refuse to let go of or lose. In both cases, we indulge imagination. Whatever notions we hold of time and space beyond our present reality belong to God, to mystery, and as such, are beyond our knowing and our control. Imaginings seem a flimsy basis for confidence; Jesus rarely indulged those who persisted in validating their fantasies, but instead reminded on several occasions that knowledge of time and space beyond the present is not ours to know.

Still, we are creatures endowed with imagination. How might our ability to imagine be put to God's service? How might our ability to imagine shape our responses to conform to God's creative will for human being?

Imagine heaven as eternal life in our enjoyment of God, the fulfillment of profound relationship with God. As such, heaven is neither time nor space, but is quality of relationship, full participation in the life and love of God. This is not so difficult to imagine if we draw upon the analogy of our deepest friendships. In those few and very special relationships many of us have been privileged to know, we experience relationship as unbounded by time or space. In the company of such friends, even when only occasionally met, the passage of years dissolves; conversation seems to resume where it last left off. Even when separated, a thought or letter or voice can transcend the distance and we are present with the friend as if bodies were inconsequential.

Imagine hell as eternal death, profound rejection of God. As such, hell is neither time nor space, but is the antithesis of relationship—refusal, denial of God's life and love. This is not difficult to imagine if we draw upon the analogy of our most profound introversion. In those times that many of us have experienced, we want little more than to be left alone. In the splendor of isolation, even only occasionally indulged, time belongs to us; we have all to ourselves. Even when surrounded by others, we can transcend their proximity and absent ourselves from them as if bodies were inconsequential.

As regards life beyond this one I confess to universalism: I imagine us all in the same place. To imagine otherwise presumes too much judgment to myself, allows me to decide between whom I shall love, whom I shall dismiss or reject. I prefer the challenge of universalism, for it denies me the easy assumptions that pander to my own sin. Moreover, it accords with certain of Jesus' own notions of God's realm.

Christians pray for the dead still held in love because we trust that in God's presence they continue to grow in God's love, that neither our relationship with them nor their relationship with God is abrogated by death. Christians differ in their perception of a last judgment though we confess that the coming of the Christ is always an accounting for our lives, for the shape of our human being is always held to the standard of his. Nevertheless, we also affirm the prodigal mercy of God, whose justice is not like our justice, whose love is not like our love. God's justice and God's love surpass all our limited notions or experiences of justice and love, and extend to embrace all God's beloved, living and dead.

Central to our experience of God's justice and love is the Christian belief in the resurrection of the body, that in whatever life may lie beyond death the fullness of our being remains intact. Because we are bounded, bodied creatures, we have no better way to express the profound worth of personhood. Even the apostle Paul, whose imagination was breathtakingly expansive and capacious, found no better expression than this to communicate the unique and essential preciousness of our individuality.

While Paul confessed he had no idea what our resurrected body might look like, he was persuaded that just as one is known by the distinction of one's corporeal reality—that every name, no matter how many times repeated in successive generations, belongs to a unique face—so shall we be known to God in any life to come. His conviction is confirmed in the story of the raising of Lazarus (John 11). Fully three days in the tomb and thus certifiably dead, Lazarus comes forth from his tomb in response only to his name. Jesus does not enter the tomb to touch Lazarus, but stands outside and calls him by name. No wonder those present were filled with fear; here was evidence that human accountability survives death. The slate is not wiped clean; we do not dissolve into nothingness. A living Lazarus is both the best of news and the worst of news.

A living Lazarus is the happy news of the communion of saints, the continuing life of the whole family of God, the living and the dead, those whom we love and those whom we hurt, bound together in Christ by sacrament, prayer, and praise. A living Lazarus is the frightening news of everlasting life, of a new existence, in which we are united with all the people of God, fully knowing God and each other.

Reunion with *all* the people of God, those whom we love and those whom we hurt, newly endowed with the fullness of knowledge denied in Eden, holds potentials both dreadful and delightful. And it lends deeper meaning to the paradigm of human being realized in Jesus, the Christ.

Jesus incarnates and encourages an open, indiscriminate love; love even—especially—of our enemies. He acknowledges that this love is counterintuitive, countercultural, even contrary to the self-seeking, self-preserving bent in human nature. Yet, those who embrace this love and practice it approach the realm of God. For them the kingdom of God, says Jesus, is near. To live this way is not simply to anticipate but to participate in God's life. To live this way is to advance beyond belief and to enter hope, to live as though the promised realm of God is indeed real, here and now.

For those who have so learned to love, and to live, life in God—life in and among all the people of God—shall be filled with all the riches of relationship, including reunion and renewal of loves previously separated by death, and of friendships denied by history's limitations. I can conceive of no richer heaven. For those who resist the love held out to them and persist in withholding their love from others—for those who wish only and eternally to be left alone—I can imagine no more excruciating hell.

The apostle Paul was well acquainted with all the fearsome stuff that life can throw at us, and all the crap we're capable of inflicting on ourselves and one another. Near the end of his life, he summarized his gospel in a simple testimony to our inclusion in God's love when he wrote, "neither death, nor life, nor angels, nor principalities, nor things present, nor things to come, nor powers, nor height, nor depth, nor anything else in all creation, will be able to separate us from the love of God in Christ Jesus our Lord" (Romans 8:38–39). Christians live in the constant company of the Christ who, having experienced the worst the world can mete out, accompanies each one of us in every moment now and always, with the assurance, "Do not be afraid." In that assurance, and the love of God embodied in it, I believe.

Afterword

THIS IS THE STORY of catechism, of the catechized. The people of Pentecost are the first generation of the Christian catechized. *Catechize*, literally, "to din into," "resound," "echo." The din of Pentecost was more than the sound of Parthians, Medes, Elamites, Mesopotamians, Judeans, Cappadocians, Pontians, Asians, Phrygians, Pamphylians, Egyptians, Libyans, Roman Jews and proselytes, Cretans and Arabs all exclaiming simultaneously, enthusiastically in their own tongues the mighty works of God. The din of the catechized was the echo of their own experiences and histories colliding with generations of stories of believers before them. The din of the catechized was the resounding truth echoing off the hard realities of their own lives.

More than imparted information, ingested process, academic prowess, the outcome of catechism and catechesis is the din of the catechized. The din of the catechized is the gospel conclusion and the conclusive gospel articulated by Paul in the eighth chapter of his epistle to the church at Rome, the echo of God's great deeds in his own hard, willful life—the ultimate realization of every believer brought back into full relationship with the God who made us, the realization that go where we will, do what we may, despite all that we are or can be, God will never forsake us, never stop loving us. Nothing can ever change that. God loves us beyond all reason, beyond all justice.

God has made us, God has made us a home, God has made us a promise. The covenant is everlasting, the light is always on, the door is always open.

Comparative Contents